AF753687

The Transactional Document Guide for Business Organizations

The Transactional Document Guide for Business Organizations

Second Edition

Edited by Donald Scotten

University of Southern California

cognella

SAN DIEGO

Bassim Hamadeh, CEO and Publisher
Carrie Montoya, Manager, Revisions and Author Care
Kaela Martin, Project Editor
Christian Berk, Production Editor
Jess Estrella, Senior Graphic Designer
Alexa Lucido, Licensing Manager
Natalie Piccotti, Director of Marketing
Kassie Graves, Senior Vice President of Editorial
Jamie Giganti, Director of Academic Publishing

Copyright © 2021 by Cognella, Inc. All rights reserved. No part of this publication may be reprinted, reproduced, transmitted, or utilized in any form or by any electronic, mechanical, or other means, now known or hereafter invented, including photocopying, microfilming, and recording, or in any information retrieval system without the written permission of Cognella, Inc. For inquiries regarding permissions, translations, foreign rights, audio rights, and any other forms of reproduction, please contact the Cognella Licensing Department at rights@cognella.com.

Trademark Notice: Product or corporate names may be trademarks or registered trademarks and are used only for identification and explanation without intent to infringe.

Cover image copyright © 2018 Depositphotos/AndrewLozovyi.

Printed in the United States of America.

cognella® | CUSTOM
3970 Sorrento Valley Blvd., Ste. 500, San Diego, CA 9212

Contents

Preface

THIS BOOK IS a supplement for any introductory business organizations course. Its purpose is to expose students to authentic examples to give a sense of the strategic decisions and deals made by transactional attorneys.

The sample documents and agreements selected reflect only a portion of those commonly produced during a business entity's life-cycle. While they have been chosen for their quality, they have not been included necessarily as ideal models. Each document and agreement was shaped by particular business circumstances and is the outcome of a process.

I wish to thank my research assistant, Chris White, whose effort and advice helped put this book into your hands. Additionally, I greatly appreciate the invaluable help from my research assistant, Sabrina Kumre, who assisted with editing this new addition.

SECTION I

Corporations

DOCUMENT ONE

Articles of Incorporation

CA-FORM: ARTS-GS

http://bpd.cdn.sos.ca.gov/corp/pdf/articles/arts-gs.pdf

"ARTS-GS: Articles of Incorporation of a General Stock Corporation," https://bpd.cdn.sos.ca.gov/corp/pdf/articles/arts-gs.pdf, State of California, 2019.

ARTS-GS

Secretary of State

Articles of Incorporation of a General Stock Corporation

IMPORTANT — Read Instructions before completing this form.

Filing Fee—$100.00

Copy Fees— First page $1.00; each attachment page $0.50; Certification Fee—$5.00

Note: Corporations may have to pay minimum $800 tax to the California Franchise Tax Board each year. For more information, go to ftb.ca.gov.

This Space For Office Use Only

1. Corporate Name (Go to www.sos.ca.gov/business/be/name-availability for general corporate name requirements and restrictions.)

The name of the corporation is ______________________________

____

2. Business Addresses (Enter the **complete** business addresses.)

a. Initial Street Address of Corporation— **Do not list a P.O. Box**	City (no abbreviations)	State	Zip Code
b. Initial Mailing Address of Corporation, **if different than item 2a**	City (no abbreviations)	State	Zip Code

3. Service of Process (Must provide either Individual **OR** Corporation.)

INDIVIDUAL—Complete Items 3a and 3b only. Must include agent's full name and California street address.

a. California Agent's First Name (if agent is **not** a corporation)	Middle Name	Last Name	Suffix
b. Street Address (if agent is not a corporation)— **Do not enter a P.O. Box**	City (no abbreviations)	State **CA**	Zip Code

CORPORATION - Complete Item 3c. Only include the name of the registered agent Corporation.

c. California Registered Corporate Agent's Name (if agent is a corporation)—Do not complete Item 3a or 3b

4. Shares (Enter the **number of shares** the corporation is authorized to issue. **Do not** leave blank or enter zero (0).)

This corporation is authorized to issue only one class of shares of stock.
The total number of shares which this corporation is authorized to issue is ______________ .

5. Purpose Statement (Do not alter the Purpose Statement.)

The purpose of the corporation is to engage in any lawful act or activity for which a corporation may be organized under the General Corporation Law of California other than the banking business, the trust company business or the practice of a profession permitted to be incorporated by the California Corporations Code.

6. Read and Sign Below (This form must be signed by each incorporator. **See instructions for signature requirements.**)

______________________________ ______________________________

Signature Type or Print Name

ARTS-GS (REV06/2019)

2019 California Secretary of State
bizfile.sos.ca.gov

DOCUMENT TWO

Restated Certificate of Incorporation (Facebook, Inc.)

10-Q 2012-08-06 EX-3.(A)

https://s21.q4cdn.com/399680738/files/doc_downloads/governance_documents/FB_CertificateOf Incorporation.pdf

Delaware

The First State

I, JEFFREY W. BULLOCK, SECRETARY OF STATE OF THE STATE OF DELAWARE, DO HEREBY CERTIFY THE ATTACHED IS A TRUE AND CORRECT COPY OF THE RESTATED CERTIFICATE OF "FACEBOOK, INC.", FILED IN THIS OFFICE ON THE TWENTY-SECOND DAY OF MAY, A.D. 2012, AT 8:10 O'CLOCK A.M.

A FILED COPY OF THIS CERTIFICATE HAS BEEN FORWARDED TO THE NEW CASTLE COUNTY RECORDER OF DEEDS.

3835815 8100
120604297

You may verify this certificate online at corp.delaware.gov/ authver.shtml

Jeffrey W. Bullock, Secretary of State
AUTHENTICATION: 9587397
DATE: 05-22-12

"Facebook, Inc. Restated Certification of Incorporation," https://s21.q4cdn.com/399680738/files/doc_downloads/governance_documents/FB_CertificateOfIncorporation.pdf, State of Delaware, 2012.

State of Delaware
Secretary of State
Division or Corporations
Delivered 08:18 AM 05/22/2012
FILED 08:10 AM 05/22/2012
SRV 120604297—3835815 FILE

Facebook, Inc.
RESTATED CERTIFICATE OF INCORPORATION

Facebook, Inc., a Delaware corporation, hereby certifies as follows.

1. The name of the corporation is Facebook, Inc. The date of filing its original Certificate of Incorporation with the Secretary of State was July 29, 2004, under the name The Facebook, Inc.

2. The Restated Certificate of Incorporation of the corporation attached hereto as Exhibit A, which is incorporated herein by this reference, and which restates, integrates and further amends the provisions of the Certificate of Incorporation of this corporation as heretofore amended and/or restated, has been duly adopted by the corporation's Board of Directors and by the stockholders in accordance with Sections 242 and 245 of the General Corporation Law of the State of Delaware, with the approval of the corporation's stockholders having been given by written consent without a meeting in accordance with Section 228 of the General Corporation Low of the State of Delaware.

IN WITNESS WHEREOF, this corporation has caused this Restated Certificate of Incorporation to be signed by its duly authorized officer and the foregoing facts stated herein are true and correct.

Dated: May 22, 2012

FACEBOOK, INC.

By: ______

Name: Mark Zuckerberg

Title: Chief Executive Officer

EXHIBIT A

FACEBOOK, INC.
RESTATED CERTIFICATE OF INCORPORATION

ARTICLE I: NAME

The name of the corporation is Facebook, Inc.

ARTICLE II: AGENT FOR SERVICE OF PROCESS

The address of the corporation's registered office in the State of Delaware is 2711 Centerville Road, Suite 400, Wilmington, County of New Castle, 19808. The name of the registered agent of the corporation at that address is Corporation Service Company.

ARTICLE III: PURPOSE

The purpose of the corporation is to engage in any lawful act or activity for which corporations may be organized under the General Corporation Law of the State of Delaware ("***General Corporation Law***").

ARTICLE IV: AUTHORIZED STOCK

1. **Total Authorized.**

The total number of shares of all classes of capital stock that the corporation has authority to issue is 9,241,000,000 shares, consisting of: 5,000,000,000 shares of Class A Common Stock, $0.000006 par value per share ("*Class A Common Stock*"), 4,141,000,000 shares of Class B Common Stock, $0.000006 par value per share ("***Class B Common Stock***" and together with the Class A Common Stock, the "***Common Stock***") and 100,000,000 shares of Preferred Stock, $0.000006 par value per share. The number of authorized shares of Class A Common Stock or Class B Common Stock may be increased or decreased (but not below the number of shares thereof then outstanding) by the affirmative vote of the holders of capital stock representing a majority of the voting power of all the then-outstanding shares of capital stock of the corporation entitled to vote thereon, irrespective of the provisions of Section 242(b)(2) of the General Corporation Law.

2. **Designation of Additional Shares**

2.1 The Board of Directors is authorized, subject to any limitations prescribed by the laws of the State of Delaware, by resolution or resolutions, to provide for the issuance of the shares of Preferred Stock in one or more series, and, by filing a certificate of designation pursuant to the applicable law of the State of Delaware ("***Certificate of Designation***"), to establish from time to time the number of shares to be included in each such series, to fix the designation, powers (including voting powers), preferences and relative, participating, optional or other rights, if any, of the shares of each such series and any qualifications, limitations or restrictions thereof, and to increase (but not above the total number of authorized shares of such class) or decrease (but not below the number of shares of such series then outstanding) the number of shares of any such series. The number of authorized shares of Preferred Stock may also be increased or decreased (but not below the number of shares thereof then outstanding) by the affirmative vote of the holders of a majority of the voting power of all the then-outstanding shares of capital stock of the corporation entitled to vote thereon, without a separate vote of the holders of the Preferred Stock or any series thereof, irrespective of the provisions of Section 242(b)(2) of the General Corporation Law, unless a vote of any such holders is required pursuant to the terms of any Certificate of Designation designating a series of Preferred Stock.

2.2 Except as otherwise expressly provided in any Certificate of Designation designating any series of Preferred Stock pursuant to the foregoing provisions of this ARTICLE IV, any new series of Preferred Stock may be designated, fixed and determined as provided herein by the Board of Directors without approval of the holders of Common Stock or the holders of Preferred Stock, or any series thereof, and any such new series may have powers, preferences and rights, including, without limitation, voting powers, dividend rights, liquidation rights, redemption rights and conversion rights, senior to, junior to or pari passu with the rights of the Common Stock, the Preferred Stock, or any future class or series of Preferred Stock or Common Stock.

3. **Rights of Class A Common Stock and Class B Common Stock.**

3.1 Equal Status. Except as otherwise provided in this Restated Certificate of Incorporation or required by applicable law, shares of Class A

Common Stock and Class B Common Stock shall have the same rights and powers, rank equally (including as to dividends and distributions, and upon any liquidation, dissolution or winding up of the corporation), share ratably and be identical in all respects and as to all matters.

3.2 Voting Rights. Except as otherwise expressly provided by this Restated Certificate of Incorporation or as provided by law, the holders of shares of Class A Common Stock and Class B Common Stock shall (a) at all times vote together as a single class on all matters (including the election of directors) submitted to a vote or for the consent (if action by written consent of the stockholders is permitted at such time under this Restated Certificate of Incorporation) of the stockholders of the corporation, (b) be entitled to notice of any stockholders' meeting in accordance with the Bylaws of the corporation and (c) be entitled to vote upon such matters and in such manner as may be provided by applicable law. Except as otherwise expressly provided herein or required by applicable law, each holder of Class A Common Stock shall have the right to one (1) vote per share of Class A Common Stock held of record by such holder and each holder of Class B Common Stock shall have the right to ten (10) votes per share of Class B Common Stock held of record by such holder.

3.3 Dividend and Distribution Rights. Shares of Class A Common Stock and Class B Common Stock shall be treated equally, identically and ratably, on a per share basis, with respect to any dividends or distributions as may be declared and paid from time to time by the Board of Directors out of any assets of the corporation legally available therefor; *provided, however,* that in the event a dividend is paid in the form of shares of Class A Common Stock or Class B Common Stock (or rights to acquire such shares), then holders of Class A Common Stock shall receive shares of Class A Common Stock (or rights to acquire such shares, as the case may be) and holders of Class B Common Stock shall receive shares of Class B Common Stock (or rights to acquire such shares, as the case may be), with holders of shares of Class A Common Stock and Class B Common Stock receiving, on a per share basis, an identical number of shares of Class A Common Stock or Class B Common Stock, as applicable. Notwithstanding the foregoing, the Board of Directors may pay or make a disparate dividend or distribution per share of Class A Common Stock or Class B Common Stock (whether in the amount of such dividend or distribution payable per share, the form in which such dividend or distribution is payable, the timing of the payment, or otherwise) if such disparate dividend or distribution is approved in advance by the affirmative vote (or written consent if action by written consent of stockholders is permitted at such time under this Restated Certificate of incorporation) of the holders of a majority of the outstanding shares of Class A Common Stock and Class B Common Stock, each voting separately as a class.

3.4 Subdivisions, Combinations or Reclassifications. Shares of Class A Common Stock or Class B Common Stock may not be subdivided, combined or reclassified unless the shares of the other class are concurrently therewith proportionately subdivided, combined or reclassified in a manner that maintains the same proportionate equity ownership between the holders of the outstanding Class A Common Stock and Class B Common Stock on the record date for such subdivision, combination or reclassification; *provided, however,* that shares of one such class may be subdivided, combined or reclassified in a different or disproportionate manner if such subdivision, combination or reclassification is approved in advance by the affirmative vote (or written consent if action by written consent of stockholders is permitted at such time under this Restated Certificate of Incorporation) of the holders of a majority of the outstanding shares of Class A Common Stock and Class B Common Stock, each voting separately as a class.

3.5 Liquidation, Dissolution or Winding Up. Subject to the preferential or other rights of any holders of Preferred Stock then outstanding, upon the dissolution, liquidation or winding up of the corporation, whether voluntary or involuntary, holders of Class A Common Stock and Class B Common Stock will be entitled to receive ratably all assets of the corporation available for distribution to its stockholders unless disparate or different treatment of the shares of each such class with respect to distributions upon any such liquidation, dissolution or winding up is approved in advance by the affirmative vote (or written consent if action by written consent of stockholders is permitted at such time under this Restated Certificate of Incorporation) of the holders of a majority of the outstanding shares of Class A Common Stock and Class B Common Stock, each voting separately as a class.

3.6 Merger or Consolidation. In the case of any distribution or payment in respect of the shares of Class A Common Stock or Class B Common Stock upon the consolidation or merger of the Corporation with or into any other entity, or in the case of any other transaction having an effect on stockholders substantially similar to that resulting from a consolidation or merger, such distribution or payment shall be made ratably on a per share basis among the holders of the Class A Common Stock and Class B Common Stock as a single class; *provided, however,* that shares of one such class may receive different or disproportionate distributions or payments in connection with such merger, consolidation or other transaction if (i) the only difference in the per share distribution to the holders of the Class A Common Stock and Class B Common Stock is that any securities distributed to the holder of a share Class B Common Stock have ten times the voting power of any securities distributed to the holder of a share of Class A Common Stock, or (ii) such merger, consolidation or other transaction is approved by the affirmative vote (or written consent if action by written consent of stockholders is permitted at such time under this Restated Certificate of Incorporation) of the holders of a majority of the outstanding shares of Class A Common Stock and Class B Common Stock, each voting separately as a class.

3.7 Change of Control Class B Vote. Until the first date on which the outstanding shares of Class B Common Stock represent less than thirty-five percent (35%) of the total voting power of the then outstanding shares of the corporation then entitled to vote generally in the election of directors, the corporation shall not consummate a Change in Control Transaction (as defined in Section 4 of this ARTICLE IV) without first obtaining the affirmative vote (or written consent if action by written consent of stockholders is permitted at such time under this Restated Certificate of Incorporation) of the holders of a majority of the then outstanding shares of Class B Common Stock, voting as a separate class, in addition to any other vote required by applicable law, this Restated Certificate of Incorporation or the Bylaws.

3.8 Conversion of Class B Common Stock.

(a) Voluntary Conversion. Each share of Class B Common Stock shall be convertible into one (1) fully paid and nonassessable share of Class A Common Stock at the option of the holder thereof at any time upon written notice to the corporation. Before any holder of Class B Common Stock shall be entitled to voluntarily convert any shares of such Class B Common Stock, such holder shall surrender the certificate or certificates therefor (if any), duly endorsed, at the principal corporate office of the corporation or of any transfer agent for the Class B Common Stock, and shall give written notice to the corporation at its principal corporate office, of the election to convert the same and shall state therein the name or names (i) in which the certificate or certificates representing the shares of Class A Common Stock into which the shares of Class B Common Stock are so converted are to be issued if such shares are certificated or (ii) in which such shares are to be registered in book entry if such shares are uncertificated. The corporation shall, as soon as practicable thereafter, issue and deliver at such office to such holder of Class B Common Stock, or to the nominee or nominees of such holder, a certificate or certificates representing the number of shares of Class A Common Stock to which such holder shall be entitled as aforesaid (if such shares are certificated) or, if such shares are uncertificated, register such shares in book-entry form. Such conversion shall be deemed to have been made immediately prior to the close of business on the date of such surrender of the shares of Class B Common Stock to be converted following or contemporaneously with the written notice of such holder's election to convert required by this Section 3.8(a), and the person or persons entitled to receive the shares of Class A Common Stock issuable upon such conversion shall be treated for all purposes as the record holder or holders of such shares of Class A Common Stock as of such date. Each share of Class B Common Stock that is converted pursuant to this Section 3.8(a) shall be retired by the corporation and shall not be available for reissuance.

(b) Automatic Conversion. (i) Each share of Class B Common Stock shall be automatically, without further action by the holder thereof, converted into one (1) fully paid and nonassessable share of Class A Common Stock, upon the occurrence of a Transfer (as defined in Section 4 of this ARTICLE IV), other than a Permitted Transfer (as defined in Section 4 of this ARTICLE IV), of such share of Class B Common Stock and (ii) all shares of Class B Common Stock shall be automatically, without further action by any holder thereof, convened into an identical number of shares of Class A Common Stock at such date and time, or the occurrence of an event, specified by the affirmative vote (or written consent if action by written consent of stockholders is permitted at such time under this Restated Certificate of Incorporation) of the holders of a majority of the then outstanding shares Class B Common Stock, voting as a separate class (the occurrence of an event described in clause (i) or (ii) of this Section 3.8(b), a "***Conversion Event***"). Each outstanding stock certificate that, immediately prior to a Conversion Event, represented one or more shares of Class B Common Stock subject to such Conversion Event shall, upon such Conversion Event, be deemed to represent an equal number of shares of Class A Common Stock, without the need for surrender or exchange thereof. The corporation shall, upon the request of any holder whose shares of Class B Common Stock have been converted into shares of Class A Common Stock as a result of a Conversion Event and upon surrender by such holder to the corporation of the outstanding certificate(s) formerly representing such holder's shares of Class B Common Stock (if any), issue and deliver to such holder certificate(s) representing the shares of Class A Common Stock into which such holder's shares of Class B Common Stock were converted as a result of such Conversion Event (if such shares are certificated) or, if such shares are uncertificated, register such shares in book-entry form. Each share of Class B Common Stock that is converted pursuant to this Section 3.8(b) of ARTICLE IV shall thereupon be retired by the corporation and shall not be available for reissuance.

(c) The corporation may, from time to time, establish such policies and procedures, not in violation of applicable law or the other provisions of this Restated Certificate, relating to the conversion of the Class B Common Stock into Class A Common Stock, as it may deem necessary or advisable in connection therewith. If the corporation has reason to believe that a Transfer giving rise to a conversion of shares of Class B Common Stock into Class A Common Stock has occurred but has not theretofore been reflected on the books of the corporation, the corporation may request that the holder of such shares furnish affidavits or other evidence to the corporation as the corporation deems necessary to determine whether a conversion of shares of Class B Common Stock to Class A Common Stock has occurred, and if such holder does not within ten (10) days after the date of such request furnish sufficient evidence to the corporation (in the manner provided in the request) to enable the corporation to determine that no such conversion has occurred, any such shares of Class B Common Stock, to the extent not previously converted, shall be automatically converted into shares of Class A Common Stock and the same shall thereupon be registered on the books and records of the corporation. In connection with any action of stockholders taken at a meeting or by written consent (if action by written consent of stockholders is permitted at such time under this Restated Certificate of Incorporation), the stock ledger of the corporation shall be presumptive evidence as to who are the stockholders entitled to vote in person or by proxy at any meeting of stockholders or in connection with any such written consent and the class or classes or series of shares held by each such stockholder and the number of shares of each class or classes or series held by such stockholder.

3.9 Reservation of Stock. The corporation shall at all times reserve and keep available out of its authorized but unissued shares of Class A Common Stock, solely for the purpose of effecting the conversion of the shares of Class B Common Stock, such number of shares of Class A Common Stock as shall from time to time be sufficient to effect the conversion of all outstanding shares of Class B Common Stock into shares of Class A Common Stock.

3.10 Protective Provision. The corporation shall not, whether by merger, consolidation or otherwise, amend, alter, repeal or waive Sections 3 or 4 of this Article IV (or adopt any provision inconsistent therewith), without first obtaining the affirmative vote (or written consent if action by written consent of stockholders is permitted at such time under this Restated Certificate of Incorporation) of the holders of a majority of the then outstanding shares of Class B Common Stock, voting as a separate class, in addition to any other vote required by applicable law, this Restated Certificate of Incorporation or the Bylaws.

4. **Definitions**. For purposes of this Restated Certificate of Incorporation:

4.1 "Change in Control Transaction" means the occurrence of any of the following events:

(a) the sale, lease, exchange, encumbrance or other disposition (other than licenses that do not constitute an effective disposition of all or substantially all of the assets of the corporation and its subsidiaries taken as a whole, and the grant of security interests in the ordinary course of business) by the corporation of all or substantially all of the corporation's assets; or

(b) the merger or consolidation of the corporation with or into any other entity, other than a merger or consolidation that, would result in the Class B Common Stock of the corporation outstanding immediately prior thereto continuing to represent (either by remaining outstanding or by being converted into voting securities of the surviving entity or its sole parent entity) more than fifty percent (50%) of the total voting power represented by the voting securities of the corporation or such surviving entity or its sole parent entity outstanding immediately after such merger or consolidation.

4.2 "Charitable Trust" means a trust that is exempt from taxation under Section 501(c)(3) of the United States Internal Revenue Code of 1986, as amended (or any successor provision thereto) (whether a determination letter with respect to such exemption is issued before, at or after the Covered Security Date), and further includes any successor entity that is exempt from taxation under Section 501(c)(3) (or any successor provision thereto) upon a conversion of, or transfer of all or substantially all of the assets of, a Charitable Trust to such successor entity (whether a determination letter with respect to such successor's exemption is issued before, at or after the conversion date).

4.3 "Covered Security Date" means May 14, 2012.

4.4 "Family Member" shall mean with respect to any natural person who is a Qualified Stockholder, the spouse, parents, grandparents, lineal descendents, siblings and lineal descendants of siblings of such Qualified Stockholder. Lineal descendants shall include adopted persons, but only so long as they are adopted during minority.

4.5 "Qualified Stockholder" shall mean (a) the registered holder of a share of Class B Common Stock as of the Covered Security Date; (b) the initial registered holder of any shares of Class B Common Stock that are originally issued by the corporation after the Covered Security Date pursuant to the exercise or conversion of options or warrants or settlement of restricted stock units (RSUs) that, in each case, are outstanding as of the Covered Security Date; (c) each natural person who Transferred shares of or equity awards for Class B Common Stock (including any option or warrant exercisable or convertible into or any RSU that can be settled in shares of Class B Common Stock) to a Permitted Entity that is or becomes a Qualified Stockholder pursuant to subclauses (a) or (b) of this Section 4.5; and (d) a Permitted Transferee.

4.6 "Parent" of an entity shall mean any entity that directly or indirectly owns or controls a majority of the voting power of the voting securities of such entity.

4.7 "Permitted Entity" shall mean with respect to a Qualified Stockholder (a) a Permitted Trust solely for the benefit of (i) such Qualified Stockholder, (ii) one or more Family Members of such Qualified Stockholder, (iii) any other Permitted Entity of such Qualified Stockholder and/or (iv) any entity that is described in Sections 501(c)(3), 170(b)(1)(A), 170(c), 2055(a) or 2522(a) of the United States Internal Revenue Code of 1986, as amended (or any successor provision thereto), (b) any general partnership, limited partnership, limited liability company, corporation or other entity exclusively owned by (i) such Qualified Stockholder, (ii) one or more Family Members of such Qualified Stockholder and/or (iii) any other Permitted Entity of such Qualified Stockholder, (c) any Charitable Trust created by a Qualified Stockholder, which Charitable Trust was (x) validly created and (y) a registered holder of shares of capital stock of the corporation, in each case prior to the Covered Security Date (whether or not it continuously holds such shares of capital stock or any other shares of capital stock of the corporation at all times before or after the Covered Security Date), (d) the personal representative of the estate of a Qualified Stockholder upon the death of such Qualified Stockholder solely to the extent the executor is acting in the capacity as personal representative of such estate, (e) a revocable living trust, which revocable living trust is itself both a Permitted Trust and a Qualified Stockholder, during the lifetime of the natural person grantor of such trust, or (f) a revocable living trust, which revocable living trust is itself both a Permitted Trust and a Qualified Stockholder, following the death of the natural person grantor of such trust, solely to the extent that such shares are held in such trust pending distribution to the beneficiaries designated in such trust. Except as explicitly provided for herein, a Permitted Entity of a Qualified Stockholder shall not cease to be a Permitted Entity of that Qualified Stockholder solely by reason of the death of that Qualified Stockholder.

4.8 "Permitted Transfer" shall mean, and be restricted to, any Transfer of a share of Class B Common Stock:

(a) by a Qualified Stockholder (or the estate of a deceased Qualified Stockholder) to (i) one or more Family Members of such Qualified Stockholder, or (ii) any Permitted Entity of such Qualified Stockholder; or (iii) to such Qualified Stockholder's revocable living trust, which revocable living trust is itself both a Permitted Trust and a Qualified Stockholder;

(b) by a Permitted Entity of a Qualified Stockholder to (i) such Qualified Stockholder or one or more Family Members of such Qualified Stockholder, or (ii) any other Permitted Entity of such Qualified Stockholder; or

(c) by a Qualified Stockholder that is a natural person or revocable living trust to an entity that is exempt from taxation under Section 501(c)(3) of the United States Internal Revenue Code of 1986, as amended (or any successor provision thereto) (a "501(c)(3) Organization") or an entity that is exempt from taxation under Section 501(c)(3) and described in Section 509(a)(3) of United States Internal Revenue Code of 1986, as amended (or any successor provision thereto) (a "Supporting Organization"), as well as any Transfer by a 501(c)(3) Organization to a Supporting Organization of which such 501(c)(3) Organization (x) is a supported organization (within the meaning of Section 509(f)(3) of the United States Internal Revenue Code of 1986, as amended (or any successor provision thereto)), and (y) has the power to appoint a majority of the board of directors, provided that such 501(c)(3) Organization or such Supporting Organization irrevocably elects, no later than the time such share of Class B Common Stock is Transferred to it, that such share of Class B Common Stock shall automatically be converted into Class A Common Stock upon the death of such Qualified Stockholder or the natural person grantor of such Qualified Stockholder.

4.9 "Permitted Transferee" shall mean a transferee of shares of Class B Common Stock received in a Transfer that constitutes a Permitted Transfer.

4.10 "Permitted Trust" shall mean a bona fide trust where each trustee is (a) a Qualified Stockholder, (b) a Family Member of a Qualified Stockholder, (c) a professional in the business of providing trustee services, including private professional fiduciaries, trust companies and bank trust departments, or (d) solely in the case of any such trust established by a natural person grantor prior to the Covered Security Date, any other bona fide trustee.

4.11 "Transfer" of a share of Class B Common. Stock shall mean, directly or indirectly, any sale, assignment, transfer, conveyance, hypothecation or other transfer or disposition of such share or any legal or beneficial interest in such share, whether or not for value and whether voluntary or involuntary or by operation of law (including by merger, consolidation or otherwise), including, without limitation, a transfer of a share of Class B Common Stock to a broker or other nominee (regardless of whether there is a corresponding change in beneficial ownership), or the transfer of, or entering into a binding agreement with respect to, Voting Control (as defined below) over such share by proxy or otherwise. A "Transfer" shall also be deemed to have occurred with respect to a share of Class B Common Stock beneficially held by (i) an entity that is a Permitted Entity, if there occurs any act or circumstance that causes such entity to no longer be a Permitted Entity or (ii) an entity that is a Qualified Stockholder, if there occurs a Transfer on a cumulative basis, from and after the Covered Security Date, of a majority of the voting power of the voting securities of such entity or any direct or indirect Parent of such entity, other than a Transfer to parties that are, as of the Covered Security Date, holders of voting securities of any such entity or Parent of such entity. Notwithstanding the foregoing, the following shall not be considered a "Transfer" within the meaning of this ARTICLE TIV:

(a) the granting of a revocable proxy to officers or directors of the corporation at the request of the Board of Directors in connection with actions to be taken at an annual or special meeting of stockholders or in connection with any action by written consent of the stockholders solicited by the Board of Directors (if action by written consent of stockholders is permitted at such time under this Restated Certificate of Incorporation);

(b) entering into a voting trust, agreement or arrangement (with or without granting a proxy) solely with stockholders who are holders of Class B Common Stock, which voting trust, agreement or arrangement (i) is disclosed either in a Schedule 13D filed with the Securities and Exchange Commission or in writing to the Secretary of the corporation, (ii) either has a term not exceeding one (1) year or is terminable by the holder of the shares subject thereto at any time and (iii) does not involve any payment of cash, securities, property or other consideration to the holder of the shares subject thereto other than the mutual promise to vote shares in a designated manner;

(c) the pledge of shares of Class B Common Stock by a stockholder that creates a mere security interest in such shares pursuant to a bona fide loan or indebtedness transaction for so long as such stockholder continues to exercise Voting Control over such pledged shares; *provided, however,* that a foreclosure on such shares or other similar action by the pledgee shall constitute a "Transfer" unless such foreclosure or similar action qualifies as a "Permitted Transfer" at such time; or

(d) any change in the trustees or the person(s) and/or entity(ies) having or exercising Voting Control over shares of Class B Common Stock (i) of a Charitable Trust that qualifies as a Permitted Entity pursuant to ARTICLE IV, Section 4.7 above, or (ii) of a Permitted Entity *provided* that following such change such Permitted Entity continues to be a Permitted Entity pursuant to ARTICLE IV, Section 4.7 above.

4.12 "Voting Control" shall mean, with respect to a share of Class B Common Stock, the power (whether exclusive or shared) to vote or direct the voting of such share by proxy, voting agreement or otherwise.

4.13 "Voting Threshold Date" shall mean 5:00 p.m. (Eastern Time) on the first day falling on or after the date on which the outstanding shares of Class B Common Stock represent less than a majority of the total voting power of the then outstanding shares of the corporation then entitled to vote generally in the election of directors.

ARTICLE V: AMENDMENT OF BYLAWS

The Board of Directors of the corporation shall have the power to adopt, amend or repeal the Bylaws of the corporation. Any adoption, amendment or repeal of the Bylaws of the corporation by the Board of Directors shall require the approval of a majority of the Whole Board. For purposes of this Restated Certificate of Incorporation, the term "***Whole Board***" shall mean the total number of authorized directors whether or not there exist any vacancies in previously authorized directorships. The stockholders shall also have power to adopt, amend or repeal the Bylaws of the corporation. Prior to the Voting Threshold Date, in addition to any vote of the holders of any class or series of stock of the corporation required by applicable law or by this Restated Certificate of Incorporation (including any Preferred Stock issued pursuant to a Certificate of Designation), such adoption, amendment or repeal of the Bylaws of the corporation by the stockholders shall require the affirmative vote of a majority in voting power of all of the then outstanding shares of capital stock of the corporation entitled to vote generally in the election of directors, voting together as a single class. From and after the Voting Threshold Date, in addition to any vole of the holders of any class or series of stock of the corporation required by applicable law or by this Restated Certificate of Incorporation (including any Preferred Stock issued pursuant to a Certificate of Designation), such adoption, amendment or repeal of the Bylaws of the corporation by the stockholders shall require the affirmative vote of the holders of at least two-thirds of the voting power of all of the then-outstanding shares of the capital stock of the corporation entitled to vote generally in the election of directors, voting together as a single class.

ARTICLE VI: MATTERS RELATING TO THE BOARD OF DIRECTORS

1. **Director Powers**. The business and affairs of the corporation shall be managed by or under the direction of the Board of Directors. In addition to the powers and authority expressly conferred upon them by statute or by this Restated Certificate of Incorporation or the Bylaws of the corporation, the directors are hereby empowered to exercise all such powers and do all such acts and things as may be exercised or done by the corporation.
2. **Number of Directors**. Subject to the rights of the holders of any series of Preferred Stock to elect additional directors under specified circumstances, the number of directors shall be fixed from time to time exclusively by resolution adopted by a majority of the Whole Board.
3. **Classified Board**. Subject to the rights of the holders of any series of Preferred Stock to elect additional directors under specified circumstances, immediately following the Voting Threshold Dale, the directors shall be divided, with respect to the time for which they severally hold office, into three classes designated as Class I, Class II and Class III, respectively (the "***Classified Board***"). The Board of Directors may assign members of the Board of Directors in office immediately prior to the Classified Board becoming effective to the several classes of the Classified Board, which assignments shall become effective at the same time the Classified Board becomes effective. Directors shall be assigned to each class in accordance with a resolution or resolutions adopted by a majority of the Board of Directors, with the number of directors in each class to be divided as nearly equal as reasonably possible. The initial term of office of the Class I directors shall expire at the corporation's first annual meeting of stockholders following the date on which the Classified Board becomes effective, the initial term of office of the Class II directors shall expire at the corporation's second annual meeting of stockholders following the date on which the Classified Board becomes effective, and the initial term of office of the Class III directors shall expire at the corporation's third annual meeting of stockholders following the date on which the Classified Board becomes effective. At each annual meeting of stockholders following the date on which the Classified Board becomes effective, directors elected to succeed those directors of the class whose terms then expire shall be elected

for a term of office to expire at the third succeeding annual meeting of stockholders after their election.

4. **Term and Removal**. Each director shall hold office until such director's successor is elected and qualified, or until such director's earlier death, resignation or removal. Any director may resign at any time upon notice to the corporation given in writing or by any electronic transmission permitted in the corporation's Bylaws or in accordance with applicable law. Subject to the rights of the holders of any series of Preferred Stock with respect to directors elected thereby, from and after the effectiveness of the Classified Board, no director may be removed except for cause and only by the affirmative vote of the holders of at least a majority of the voting power of the then-outstanding shares of capital stock of the corporation then entitled to vote at an election of directors voting together as a single class. No decrease in the number of directors constituting the Whole Board shall shorten the term of any incumbent director.
5. **Board Vacancies**. Subject to the rights of the holders of any series of Preferred Stock to elect directors under specified circumstances, from and after the effectiveness of the Classified Board, any vacancy occurring in the Board of Directors for any cause, and any newly created directorship resulting from any increase in the authorized number of directors, shall (unless (a) the Board of Directors determines by resolution that any such vacancy or newly created directorship shall be filled by the stockholders or (b) otherwise required by applicable law) be filled only by the affirmative vote of a majority' of the directors then in office, even if less than a quorum, or by a sole remaining director, and not by the stockholders. Any director elected in accordance with the preceding sentence shall hold office for a term expiring at the annual meeting of stockholders at which the term of office of the class to which the director has been elected expires or until such director's successor shall have been duly elected and qualified.
6. **Vote by Ballot**. Election of directors need not be by written ballot.

ARTICLE VII: DIRECTOR LIABILITY; INDEMNIFICATION

1. **Limitation of Liability**. To the fullest extent permitted by law, no director of the corporation shall be personally liable to the corporation or its stockholders for monetary damages for breach of fiduciary

duty as a director. Without limiting the effect of the preceding sentence, if the General Corporation Law is hereafter amended to authorize the further elimination or limitation of the liability of a director, then the liability of a director of the corporation shall be eliminated or limited to the fullest extent permitted by the General Corporation Law, as so amended.

2. **Indemnification**. The corporation shall indemnify to the fullest extent permitted by law any person made or threatened to be made a party' to an action or proceeding, whether criminal, civil, administrative or investigative, by reason of the fact that he, his testator or intestate is or was a director or officer of the corporation or any predecessor of the Corporation, or serves or served at any other enterprise as a director or officer at the request of the corporation or any predecessor to the corporation.
3. **Change in Rights**. Neither any amendment nor repeal of this ARTICLE VII, nor the adoption of any provision of this Restated Certificate of Incorporation inconsistent with this ARTICLE VII, shall eliminate or reduce the effect of this Article VII in respect of any matter occurring, or any action or proceeding accruing or arising or that, but for this Article VII, would accrue or arise, prior to such amendment, repeal or adoption of an inconsistent provision.

ARTICLE VIII: MATTERS RELATING TO STOCKHOLDERS

1. **No Action by Written Consent of Stockholders**. Subject to the rights of the holders of any series of Preferred Stock with respect to actions by the holders of shares of such series, from and after the Voting Threshold Date, (a) no action shall be taken by the stockholders of the corporation except at a duly called annual or special meeting of stockholders and (b) no action shall be taken by the stockholders of the corporation by written consent.
2. **Special Meeting of Stockholders**. Subject to the rights of the holders of any series of Preferred Stock with respect to actions by the holders of shares of such series, special meetings of the stockholders of the corporation may be called only by the Board of Directors acting pursuant to a resolution adopted by a majority of the Whole Board, the Chief Executive Officer, President or the Chairperson of the Board, and may not be called by any other person or persons.

Business transacted at special meetings of stockholders shall be confined to the purpose or purposes stated in the notice of meeting.

3. **Advance Notice of Stockholder Nominations**. Advance notice of stockholder nominations for the election of directors of the corporation and of business to be brought by stockholders before any meeting of stockholders of the corporation shall be given in the manner provided in the Bylaws of the corporation.
4. **Business Combinations**. The corporation elects not to be governed by Section 203 of the General Corporation Law.

ARTICLE IX: CHOICE OF FORUM

Unless the corporation consents in writing to the selection of an alternative forum, the Court of Chancery of the State of Delaware shall, to the fullest extent permitted by law. be the sole and exclusive forum for (1) any derivative action or proceeding brought on behalf of the corporation, (2) any action asserting a claim of breach of a fiduciary duty owed by, or other wrongdoing by, any director, officer, employee or agent of the corporation to the corporation or the corporation's stockholders, (3) any action asserting a claim arising pursuant to any provision of the General Corporation Law or the corporation's Restated Certificate of Incorporation or Bylaws, (4) any action to interpret, apply, enforce or determine the validity of the corporation's Restated Certificate of Incorporation or Bylaws or (5) any action asserting a claim governed by the internal affairs doctrine, in each such case subject to said Court of Chancery having personal jurisdiction over the indispensable patties named as defendants therein. Any person or entity purchasing or otherwise acquiring any interest in shares of capital stock of the corporation shall be deemed to have notice of and consented to the provisions of this ARTICLE IX.

ARTICLE X: AMENDMENT OF RESTATED CERTIFICATE OF INCORPORATION

The corporation reserves the right to amend or repeal any provision contained in this Restated Certificate of Incorporation in the manner prescribed by the laws of the State of Delaware and all rights conferred upon stockholders are granted subject to this reservation; *provided, however,* that, notwithstanding any other provision of this Restated Certificate of Incorporation or any provision of applicable law that might otherwise permit a lesser vole or no vote, but in addition to any vote of the holders of any class or series of the capital stock of this corporation required by applicable law or by this Restated Certificate of Incorporation, from and after the Voting Threshold Date, any amendment to or repeal of this ARTICLE X or ARTICLE V, ARTICLE VI, ARTICLE VII, ARTICLE VIII or ARTICLE IX of this Restated Certificate of Incorporation (or the adoption of any provision inconsistent therewith) shall require the affirmative vote of the holders of at least two-thirds of the voting power of the then outstanding shares of capital stock of the corporation entitled to vote generally in the election of directors, voting together as a single class.

****

DOCUMENT THREE

Bylaws (Facebook, Inc.)

8-K 2015-10-28 EX-3.B

https://s21.q4cdn.com/399680738/files/doc_downloads/governance_documents/2019/Facebook-Amended-Restated-Bylaws.pdf

FACEBOOK, INC.

a Delaware corporation

AMENDED AND RESTATED BYLAWS

As Amended and Restated April 10, 2019

"Facebook Inc.'s Amended and Restated Bylaws As Amended and Restated April 10, 2019," https://s21.q4cdn.com/399680738/files/doc_downloads/governance_documents/2019/Facebook-Amended-Restated-Bylaws.pdf, State of Delaware, 2019.

FACEBOOK, INC.

a Delaware corporation

AMENDED AND RESTATED BYLAWS

TABLE OF CONTENTS

FACEBOOK, INC.

a Delaware corporation

AMENDED AND RESTATED BYLAWS

As Amended and Restated April 10, 2019

ARTICLE I: STOCKHOLDERS

Section 1.1: Annual Meetings. If required by applicable law, an annual meeting of stockholders shall be held for the election of directors at such date and time as may be determined from time to time by the Board of Directors of the Corporation (the "***Board***"). The meeting may be held either at a place, within or without the State of Delaware, or by means of remote communication as the Board in its sole discretion may determine. Any other proper business may be transacted at the annual meeting.

Section 1.2: Special Meetings. Unless otherwise provided by the Certificate of Incorporation of the Corporation (the "***Certificate of Incorporation***"), special meetings of stockholders for any purpose or purposes may be called at any time by the Chairperson of the Board, the President, the Chief Executive Officer, or by a majority of the total number of authorized directors, whether or not there exist any vacancies in previously authorized directorships (the "***Whole Board***"), and may not be called by any other person or persons. Any special meeting may be held either at a place, within or without the State of Delaware, or by means of remote communication as the Board in its sole discretion may determine. The business to be conducted at a special meeting of stockholders shall be limited to the purpose or purposes for which the meeting has been called as set forth in the notice of such meeting.

Section 1.3: Notice of Meetings. Notice of all meetings of stockholders shall be given in writing or by electronic transmission in the manner provided by applicable law (including, without limitation, as set forth in Section 7.1.1 of these Bylaws) stating the place, if any, date and time of the meeting, the means of remote communications, if any, by which stockholders and proxy holders may be deemed present in person and vote at such meeting, the record date for determining the stockholders entitled to vote at the meeting, if such date is different from the record date for determining stockholders entitled to notice of the meeting, and, in the case of a special meeting, the purpose or purposes for which the meeting is called. Unless otherwise required by applicable law or the Certificate of Incorporation, such notice shall be given not less than ten (10), nor more than sixty (60), days before the date of the meeting to each stockholder of record entitled to vote at such meeting as of the record date for determining stockholders entitled to notice of the meeting.

Section 1.4: Adjournments. Any meeting of stockholders, annual or special, may adjourn from time to time, and notice need not be given of any such adjourned meeting if the time, date and place (if any) thereof and the means of remote communications (if any) by which stockholders and proxy holders may be deemed to be present in person and vote at such adjourned meeting are announced at the meeting at which the adjournment is taken; *provided, however*, that if the adjournment is for more than thirty (30) days, a notice of the adjourned meeting shall be given to each stockholder of record entitled to vote at the meeting; *provided, further*, that if after the adjournment a new record date for stockholders entitled to vote is fixed for the adjourned meeting, the Board shall fix a new record date for notice of such adjourned meeting (which record date for determining stockholders entitled to notice of such adjourned meeting shall be the same or an earlier date as that fixed for determination of stockholders entitled to vote at the adjourned meeting), and shall give notice of the adjourned meeting to each stockholder of record as of the record date so fixed for notice of such adjourned meeting. At the adjourned meeting the Corporation may transact any business that might have been transacted at the original meeting. To the fullest extent permitted by law, the Board may postpone, reschedule or cancel any previously scheduled annual or special meeting of stockholders.

Section 1.5: Quorum. Except as otherwise provided by applicable law, the Certificate of Incorporation or these Bylaws, at each meeting of stockholders the holders of a majority of the voting power of the shares of stock entitled to vote at that meeting, present in person or represented by proxy, shall constitute a quorum for the transaction of business. If such quorum shall not be present or represented at any meeting of stockholders, the chairperson of the meeting may adjourn the meeting without notice other than announcement at the meeting, until such quorum shall be present or represented by proxy. Shares of the Corporation's stock belonging to the

Corporation (or to another corporation, if a majority of the shares entitled to vote in the election of directors of such other corporation are held, directly or indirectly, by the Corporation), shall neither be entitled to vote nor counted for quorum purposes; *provided, however*, that the foregoing shall not limit the right of the Corporation or any other corporation to vote any shares of the Corporation's stock held by it in a fiduciary capacity and to count such shares for purposes of determining a quorum.

Section 1.6: Organization; Conduct of Meetings. Meetings of stockholders shall be presided over by such person as the Board may designate or, in the absence of such a person, the Chairperson of the Board, or, in the absence of such person, the Chief Executive Officer of the Corporation, or, in the absence of such person, the President of the Corporation, or, in the absence of such person, such person as may be chosen by the holders of a majority of the voting power of the shares entitled to vote who are present, in person or by proxy, at the meeting. Such person shall be chairperson of the meeting. The Board may adopt by resolution such rules and regulations for the conduct of the meeting of stockholders as it shall deem appropriate. Except to the extent inconsistent with such rules and regulations as adopted by the Board, the chairperson of the meeting shall have the right and authority to convene and, for any or no reason, to recess and/or to adjourn the meeting, to prescribe such rules, regulations and procedures and to do all such acts as in his or her judgment are appropriate for the proper conduct of the meeting. Such rules, regulations or procedures, whether adopted by the Board or prescribed by the chairperson, may include, without limitation, the following: (i) the establishment of an agenda or order of business for the meeting; (ii) rules and procedures for maintaining order at the meeting and the safety of those present; (iii) limitations on attendance at or participation in the meeting to stockholders of record of the Corporation, their duly authorized and constituted proxies or such other persons as the chairperson of the meeting shall determine; (iv) restrictions on entry to the meeting after the time fixed for the commencement thereof; and (v) limitations on the time allotted to questions or comments by participants. The chairperson of the meeting, in addition to making any other determinations that may be appropriate to the conduct of the meeting, shall, if the facts warrant, determine and declare to the meeting that a matter or business was not properly brought before the meeting and, if such chairperson should so determine, such chairperson shall so declare to the meeting and any such matter or business not properly brought before the meeting shall not be transacted or considered. The Secretary of the Corporation shall act as secretary of the meeting, but in such person's absence the chairperson of the meeting may appoint any person to act as secretary of the meeting.

Section 1.7: Voting; Proxies. Each stockholder entitled to vote at a meeting of stockholders, or to take corporate action by written consent without a meeting, may authorize another person or persons to act for such stockholder by proxy. Such a proxy may be prepared, transmitted and delivered in any manner permitted by applicable law. Except as otherwise provided by the Certificate of Incorporation, directors shall be elected by a plurality of the votes of the shares present in person or represented by proxy at the meeting and entitled to vote on the election of directors. Except as otherwise provided by applicable law, the Certificate of Incorporation or these Bylaws, or any other applicable rules or regulations, including the applicable rules or regulations of any stock exchange, every matter other than the election of directors shall be decided by the affirmative vote of a majority of the votes properly cast for or against such matter, and, for the avoidance of doubt, neither abstentions nor broker non-votes shall be counted as votes cast for or against such matter.

Section 1.8: Fixing Date for Determination of Stockholders of Record.
1.8.1 Meetings. In order that the Corporation may determine the stockholders entitled to notice of any meeting of stockholders or any adjournment thereof, the Board may fix a record date, which record date shall not precede the date upon which the resolution fixing the record date is adopted by the Board and which record date shall not be more than sixty (60), nor less than ten (10), days before the date of such meeting. If the Board so fixes such record date for notice of such meeting, such date shall also be the record date for determining the stockholders entitled to vote at such meeting unless the Board determines, at the time it fixes such record date for notice of such meeting, that a later date on or before the date of the meeting shall be the date for making such determination. If no record date is fixed by the Board, then the record date for determining stockholders entitled to notice of or to vote at a meeting of stockholders shall be at the close of business on the day next preceding the day on which notice is given. A determination of stockholders of record entitled to notice of or to vote at a meeting of stockholders shall apply to any adjournment of the meeting; *provided, however*, that the Board may fix a new record date for determination of stockholders entitled to vote at the adjourned meeting, and, in such case, shall also fix as the record date for stockholders entitled to notice of such adjourned meeting the same or an earlier date as that fixed

for determination of stockholders entitled to vote in accordance herewith at the adjourned meeting.

1.8.2 Stockholder Action by Written Consent. In order that the Corporation may determine the stockholders entitled to consent to corporate action in writing without a meeting, the Board may fix a record date, which record date shall not precede the date upon which the resolution fixing the record date is adopted by the Board, and which date shall not be more than ten (10) days after the date upon which the resolution fixing the record date is adopted by the Board. If no record date has been fixed by the Board pursuant to the first sentence of this Section 1.8.2, the record date for determining stockholders entitled to consent to corporate action in writing without a meeting, when no prior action by the Board is required by applicable law, shall be the first date on which a signed written consent setting forth the action taken or proposed to be taken is delivered to the Corporation by delivery to its registered office in Delaware, its principal place of business, or to any officer or agent of the Corporation having custody of the book in which proceedings of meetings of stockholders are recorded. If no record date has been fixed by the Board pursuant to the first sentence of this Section 1.8.2, the record date for determining stockholders entitled to consent to corporate action in writing without a meeting if prior action by the Board is required by applicable law shall be at the close of business on the date on which the Board adopts the resolution taking such prior action.

1.8.3 Other Matters. In order that the Corporation may determine the stockholders entitled to receive payment of any dividend or other distribution or allotment of any rights, or the stockholders entitled to exercise any rights in respect of any change, conversion or exchange of stock or for the purpose of any other lawful action, the Board may fix a record date, which record date shall not precede the date upon which the resolution fixing the record date is adopted, and which record date shall not be more than sixty (60) days prior to such action. If no such record date is fixed, the record date for determining stockholders for any such purpose shall be at the close of business on the day on which the Board adopts the resolution relating thereto.

Section 1.9: List of Stockholders Entitled to Vote. The Corporation shall prepare, at least ten (10) days before the date of every meeting of stockholders, a complete list of stockholders entitled to vote at the meeting; *provided, however,* if the record date for determining the stockholders entitled to vote is less than ten (10) days before the meeting date, the list shall reflect the stockholders entitled to vote as of the tenth (10th) day before the meeting date, arranged in alphabetical order and showing the address of each stockholder and the number of shares registered in the name of each stockholder. Nothing contained in this Section 1.9 shall require the Corporation to include electronic mail addresses or other electronic contact information on such list. Such list shall be open to the examination of any stockholder, for any purpose germane to the meeting, for a period of at least ten (10) days prior to the meeting, (i) on a reasonably accessible electronic network (provided that the information required to gain access to the list is provided with the notice of the meeting), or (ii) during ordinary business hours at the principal place of business of the Corporation. If the meeting is to be held at a place, the list shall also be produced and kept at the time and place of the meeting during the whole time thereof and may be inspected by any stockholder who is present at the meeting. If the meeting is held solely by means of remote communication, then the list shall be open to the examination of any stockholder during the whole time of the meeting on a reasonably accessible electronic network, and the information required to access the list shall be provided with the notice of the meeting.

Section 1.10: Action by Written Consent of Stockholders.

1.10.1 General. Unless otherwise restricted by the Certificate of Incorporation, any action required or permitted to be taken at any annual or special meeting of the stockholders may be taken without a meeting, without prior notice and without a vote, if a consent or consents in writing, setting forth the action so taken, shall be signed by the holders of outstanding stock having not less than the minimum number of votes that would be necessary to authorize or take such action at a meeting at which all shares entitled to vote thereon were present and voted and shall be delivered to the Corporation by delivery to its registered office in the State of Delaware, its principal place of business, or an officer or agent of the Corporation having custody of the book in which minutes of proceedings of stockholders are recorded. Delivery made to the Corporation's registered office shall be by hand or by certified or registered mail, return receipt requested. Prompt notice of the taking of the corporate action without a meeting by less than unanimous written consent shall, to the extent required by law, be given to those stockholders who have not consented in writing and who, if the action had been taken at a meeting, would have been entitled to notice of the meeting if the record date for notice of such meeting had been the date that written consents signed by a sufficient number of holders to take the action were delivered to the Corporation.

1.10.2 Procedures. No written consent shall be effective to take the corporate action referred to therein unless written consents signed by a sufficient number of stockholders to take action are delivered to the Corporation in the manner prescribed in this Section 1.10 and applicable law within 60 days of the first date on which a written consent is so delivered to the Corporation.

Section 1.11: Inspectors of Elections.

1.11.1 Appointment. The Corporation shall, in advance of any meeting of stockholders, appoint one or more inspectors of election to act at the meeting and make a written report thereof. The Corporation may designate one or more persons as alternate inspectors to replace any inspector who fails to act. If no inspector or alternate is able to act at a meeting of stockholders, the chairperson of the meeting shall appoint one or more inspectors to act at the meeting.

1.11.2 Inspector's Oath. Each inspector of election, before entering upon the discharge of his duties, shall take and sign an oath faithfully to execute the duties of inspector with strict impartiality and according to the best of such inspector's ability.

1.11.3 Duties of Inspectors. At a meeting of stockholders, the inspectors of election shall (a) ascertain the number of shares outstanding and the voting power of each share, (b) determine the shares represented at a meeting and the validity of proxies and ballots, (c) count all votes and ballots, (d) determine and retain for a reasonable period of time a record of the disposition of any challenges made to any determination by the inspectors, and (e) certify their determination of the number of shares represented at the meeting, and their count of all votes and ballots. The inspectors may appoint or retain other persons or entities to assist the inspectors in the performance of the duties of the inspectors.

1.11.4 Opening and Closing of Polls. The date and time of the opening and the closing of the polls for each matter upon which the stockholders will vote at a meeting shall be announced by the chairperson of the meeting at the meeting. No ballot, proxies or votes, nor any revocations thereof or changes thereto, shall be accepted by the inspectors after the closing of the polls unless the Court of Chancery of the State of Delaware upon application by a stockholder shall determine otherwise.

1.11.5 Determinations. In determining the validity and counting of proxies and ballots, the inspectors shall be limited to an examination of the proxies, any envelopes submitted with those proxies, any information provided in accordance with Section 211(e) or Section 212(c)(2) of the General Corporation Law of the State of Delaware (the "***DGCL***") or any information provided pursuant to Section 211(a)(2)b.(i) or (iii) of the DGCL, ballots and the regular books and records of the Corporation, except that the inspectors may consider other reliable information for the limited purpose of reconciling proxies and ballots submitted by or on behalf of banks, brokers, their nominees or similar persons which represent more votes than the holder of a proxy is authorized by the record owner to cast or more votes than the stockholder holds of record. If the inspectors consider other reliable information for the limited purpose permitted under the DGCL and set forth herein, the inspectors at the time they make their certification of their determinations pursuant to the relevant provisions of the DGCL set forth herein shall specify the precise information considered by them, including the person or persons from whom they obtained the information, when the information was obtained, the means by which the information was obtained and the basis for the inspectors' belief that such information is accurate and reliable.

Section 1.12: Notice of Stockholder Business; Nominations.

1.12.1 Annual Meeting of Stockholders.

a. Nominations of persons for election to the Board and the proposal of other business to be considered by the stockholders may be made at an annual meeting of stockholders only: (i) pursuant to the Corporation's notice of such meeting (or any supplement thereto), (ii) by or at the direction of the Board or any committee thereof or (iii) by any stockholder of the Corporation who was a stockholder of record at the time of giving of the notice provided for in this Section 1.12 (the "***Record Stockholder***"), who is entitled to vote at such meeting and who complies with the notice and other procedures set forth in this Section 1.12 in all applicable respects. For the avoidance of doubt, the foregoing clause (iii) shall be the exclusive means for a stockholder to make nominations or propose business (other than business included in the Corporation's proxy materials pursuant to Rule 14a-8 under the Securities Exchange Act of 1934, as amended (such act, and the rules and regulations promulgated thereunder, the "***Exchange Act***")), at an annual meeting of stockholders, and such a stockholder must fully comply with the notice and other procedures set forth in this Section 1.12 to make such nominations or propose business before an annual meeting.

b. For nominations or other business to be properly brought before an annual meeting by a Record Stockholder pursuant to Section 1.12.1(a):

   (i) the Record Stockholder must have given timely notice thereof in writing to the Secretary of the Corporation and provide any updates or supplements to such notice at the times and in the forms required by this Section 1.12;
   (ii) any such proposed business (other than the nomination of persons for election to the Board) must constitute a proper matter for stockholder action;
   (iii) if the Proposing Person (as defined below) has provided the Corporation with a Solicitation Notice (as defined below), such Proposing Person must, in the case of a proposal other than the nomination of persons for election to the Board, have delivered a proxy statement and form of proxy to holders of at least the percentage of the Corporation's voting shares required under applicable law to carry any such proposal, or, in the case of a nomination or nominations, have delivered a proxy statement and form of proxy to holders of a percentage of the Corporation's voting shares that such Proposing Person has reasonably determined to be sufficient to elect the nominee or nominees proposed to be nominated by such Record Stockholder, and must, in either case, have included in such materials the Solicitation Notice; and
   (iv) if no Solicitation Notice relating thereto has been timely provided pursuant to this Section 1.12, the Proposing Person proposing such business or nomination must not have solicited a number of proxies sufficient to have required the delivery of such a Solicitation Notice under this Section 1.12.

To be timely, a Record Stockholder's notice must be delivered to the Secretary at the principal executive offices of the Corporation not later than the close of business on the ninetieth (90th) day nor earlier than the close of business on the one hundred twentieth (120th) day prior to the first anniversary of the preceding year's annual meeting; *provided, however*, that in the event that the date of the annual meeting is more than thirty (30) days before or more than seventy (70) days after such anniversary date, notice by the Record Stockholder to be timely must be so delivered (A) no earlier than the close of business on the one hundred twentieth (120th) day prior to such annual meeting and (B) no later than the close of business on the later of the ninetieth (90th) day prior to such annual meeting or the close of business on the tenth (10th) day following the day on which Public Announcement (as defined below) of the date of such meeting is first made by the Corporation. In no event shall the adjournment or postponement of an annual meeting commence a new time period (or extend any time period) for the giving of a Record Stockholder's notice as described above. Such Record Stockholder's notice shall set forth:

(x) as to each person whom the Record Stockholder proposes to nominate for election or reelection as a director, in addition to the matters set forth in paragraph (z) below, such Record Stockholder's notice shall set forth:

  (i) the name, age, business address and residence address of such person;
  (ii) the principal occupation or employment of such person;
  (iii) the class, series and number of any shares of stock of the Corporation that are beneficially owned or owned of record by such person or any Associated Person (as defined below);
  (iv) the date or dates such shares were acquired and the investment intent of such acquisition;
  (v) a description of all direct and indirect compensation and other material monetary agreements, arrangements and understandings during the past three (3) years, and any other material relationships, between or among such Proposing Person or any of its respective affiliates and associates, on the one hand, and each proposed nominee, and his or her respective affiliates and associates, on the other hand, including all information that would be required to be disclosed pursuant to Rule 404 promulgated under Regulation S-K if the Proposing Person or any of its respective affiliates and associates were the "registrant" for purposes of such rule and the nominee were a director or executive officer of such registrant;
  (vi) a completed and signed questionnaire, representation and agreement required by Section 1.12.2 of these Bylaws;
  (vii) such person's written consent to being named in the Corporation's proxy statement as a nominee of the stockholder, to the public disclosure of information regarding or related to

such person provided to the Corporation by such person or otherwise pursuant to this Section 1.12 and to serving as a director if elected;

(viii) all information relating to such person that would be required to be disclosed in solicitations of proxies for election of directors, or would be otherwise required, in each case pursuant to and in accordance with Section 14(a) under the Exchange Act, and the rules and regulations promulgated thereunder; and

(ix) such other information as the Corporation may reasonably require to determine whether such person meets the independence requirements of the stock exchange upon which the capital stock of the Corporation is primarily traded or the eligibility of such proposed nominee to serve as a director of the Corporation.

(y) as to any business other than the nomination of a director or directors that the Record Stockholder proposes to bring before the meeting, in addition to the matters set forth in paragraph (z) below, such Record Stockholder's notice shall set forth: (i) a brief description of the business desired to be brought before the meeting, the text of the proposal or business (including the text of any resolutions proposed for consideration and in the event that such business includes a proposal to amend the Bylaws, the text of the proposed amendment), the reasons for conducting such business at the meeting and any material interest in such business of such Proposing Person, if any, including any anticipated benefit to the Proposing Person; and (ii) a description of all agreements, arrangements and understandings between or among any such Proposing Person and any of its respective affiliates or associates, on the one hand, and any other person or persons, on the other hand, (including their names) in connection with the proposal of such business by such Proposing Person;

(z) as to each Proposing Person giving the notice, such Record Stockholder's notice shall set forth:

(i) the name and address of such Proposing Person, including, if applicable, their name and address as they appear on the Corporation's stock ledger, if different;

(ii) the class or series and number of shares of capital stock of the Corporation that are directly or indirectly owned beneficially and of record by such Proposing Person, including any shares of any class or series of capital stock of the Corporation as to which such Proposing Person has a right to acquire beneficial ownership at any time in the future;

(iii) whether and the extent to which any derivative interest in the Corporation's equity securities (including without limitation any option, warrant, convertible security, stock appreciation right, or similar right with an exercise or conversion privilege or a settlement payment or mechanism at a price related to any class or series of shares of the Corporation or with a value derived in whole or in part from the value of any class or series of shares of the Corporation, whether or not such instrument or right shall be subject to settlement in shares of the underlying class or series of capital stock of the Corporation or otherwise, and any cash-settled equity swap, total return swap, synthetic equity position or similar derivative arrangement (any of the foregoing, a "Derivative Instrument"), as well as any rights to dividends on the shares of any class or series of capital stock of the Corporation that are separated or separable from the underlying shares of capital stock of the Corporation) or any short interest in any security of the Corporation (for purposes of this Bylaw a person shall be deemed to have a short interest in a security if such person directly or indirectly, through any contract, arrangement, understanding, relationship or otherwise, has the opportunity to profit or share in any profit derived from any increase or decrease in the value of the subject security, including through performance-related fees) is held directly or indirectly by or for the benefit of such Proposing Person, including without limitation whether and the extent to which any ongoing hedging or other transaction or series of transactions has been entered into by or on behalf of, or any other agreement, arrangement or understanding (including without limitation any short position or any borrowing or lending of shares) has been made, the effect or intent of which is to mitigate loss to, or manage risk or benefit of share price changes for, or to increase or decrease the voting power of, such Proposing Person with respect to securities of the Corporation (any of the foregoing, a "Short Interest");

(iv) any proportionate interest in shares of capital stock of the Corporation or Derivative Instruments held, directly or indirectly, by a general or limited partnership in which such Proposing Person or any of its respective affiliates or associates is a general partner or, directly or indirectly, beneficially owns an interest in a general partner of such general or limited partnership;

(v) any significant equity interests or any Derivative Instruments or Short Interests in any Competitor (as defined below) held by such Proposing Person and/or any of its respective affiliates or associates;

(vi) any proxy, contract, arrangement, or relationship pursuant to which the Proposing Person has a right to vote, directly or indirectly, any shares of capital stock or other voting security of the Corporation;

(vii) a written description of any direct or indirect material interest in any material contract or agreement with the Corporation, any affiliate of the Corporation or any Competitor (including, in any such case, any employment agreement, collective bargaining agreement or consulting agreement);

(viii) a written description of any agreement, arrangement or understanding (whether oral or written) with respect to the nomination or proposal (including any knowledge that another person or entity is Acting in Concert (defined below) with such Proposing Person) between or among such Proposing Person, any of its respective affiliates or associates and any others Acting in Concert with the foregoing, including, in the case of a nomination, the nominee;

(ix) a written description of any other material relationship between such Proposing Person, on the one hand, and the Corporation, any affiliate of the Corporation or any Competitor, on the other hand;

(x) a representation that the Record Stockholder is a holder of record of stock of the Corporation entitled to vote at such meeting and intends to appear in person or by proxy at the meeting to propose such business or nomination;

(xi) a representation whether such Proposing Person intends (or is part of a group that intends) to deliver a proxy statement and/or form of proxy to holders of, in the case of a proposal, at least the percentage of the Corporation's voting shares required under applicable law to carry the proposal or, in the case of a nomination or nominations, a sufficient number of holders of the Corporation's voting shares that the Proposing Person has reasonably determined to be sufficient to elect such nominee or nominees (an affirmative statement of such intent being a "Solicitation Notice");

(xii) such Proposing Person's written consent to the public disclosure of information provided to the Corporation pursuant to this Section 1.12; and

(xiii) any other information relating to such Proposing Person, if any, required to be disclosed in a proxy statement or other filings required to be made in connection with solicitations of proxies for, as applicable, the proposal and/or for the election of directors in an election contest pursuant to and in accordance with Section 14(a) of the Exchange Act and the rules and regulations promulgated thereunder or any information that would be required to be set forth in a Schedule 13D filed pursuant to Rule 13d-1(a) or an amendment pursuant to Rule 13d-2(a) if such a statement were required to be filed under the Exchange Act and the rules and regulations promulgated thereunder by such Proposing Person and/or any of its respective affiliates or associates.

c. A stockholder providing written notice required by this Section 1.12 shall update such notice in writing, if necessary, so that the information provided or required to be provided in such notice is true and correct in all material respects as of (i) the record date for determining the stockholders entitled to notice of the meeting and (ii) the close of business on the tenth (10th) business day prior to the meeting or any adjournment or postponement thereof. In the case of an update pursuant to clause (i) of the foregoing sentence, such update shall be received by the Secretary of the Corporation at the principal executive office of the Corporation not later than five (5) business days after the record date for determining the stockholders entitled to notice of the meeting, and in the case of an update and supplement pursuant to clause (ii) of the foregoing sentence, such update and supplement shall be received by the Secretary of the Corporation at the principal executive office of the Corporation not later than eight (8) business days prior to the date for the meeting and, if practicable, any adjournment or postponement thereof (and, if not practicable, on the first practicable date prior to the date to which the meeting has been adjourned or postponed). For the avoidance of doubt, the obligation to update as set forth in this paragraph shall not limit the Corporation's rights with respect to any deficiencies in any notice provided by a stockholder, extend any applicable deadlines hereunder or enable or be deemed to permit a stockholder who has previously submitted notice hereunder to amend or update any proposal or nomination or to submit any new proposal, including by changing or adding nominees, matters, business and/or resolutions proposed to be brought before a meeting of the stockholders.

d. Notwithstanding anything this Section 1.12 to the contrary, in the event that the number of directors to be elected to the Board is increased effective after the time period for which nominations would otherwise be due under Section 1.12.1(b) and there is no Public Announcement by the Corporation naming the nominees for the additional directorships at least one hundred (100) days prior to the first anniversary of the preceding year's annual meeting, a stockholder's notice required by this Section 1.12 shall also be considered timely, but only with respect to nominees for the additional directorships, if it shall be delivered to the Secretary of the Corporation at the principal executive office of the Corporation no later than the close of business on the tenth (10th) day following the day on which such Public Announcement is first made by the Corporation.

1.12.2 Submission of Questionnaire, Representation and Agreement. To be eligible to be a nominee of any stockholder for election or reelection as a director of the Corporation, the person proposed to be nominated must deliver (in accordance with the time periods prescribed for delivery of notice under Section 1.12 of these Bylaws) to the Secretary at the principal executive offices of the Corporation a completed and signed questionnaire in the form required by the Corporation (which form the stockholder shall request in writing from the Secretary of the Corporation and which the Secretary shall provide to such stockholder within ten days of receiving such request) with respect to the background and qualification of such person to serve as a director of the Corporation and the background of any other person or entity on whose behalf, directly or indirectly, the nomination is being made and a signed representation and agreement (in the form available from the Secretary upon written request) that such person: (a) is not and will not become a party to (i) any agreement, arrangement or understanding with, and has not given any commitment or assurance to, any person or entity as to how such person, if elected as a director of the Corporation, will act or vote on any issue or question (a "***Voting Commitment***") that has not been disclosed to the Corporation or (ii) any Voting Commitment that could limit or interfere with such person's ability to comply, if elected as a director of the Corporation, with such person's fiduciary duties under applicable law, (b) is not and will not become a party to any Compensation Arrangement (as defined below) that has not been disclosed therein, (c) if elected as a director of the Corporation, will comply with all informational and similar requirements of applicable insurance policies and laws and regulations in connection with service or action as a director of the Corporation, (d) if elected as a director of the Corporation, will comply with all corporate governance, conflict of interest, stock ownership requirements, confidentiality and trading policies and guidelines of the Corporation publicly disclosed from time to time, (e) if elected as a director of the Corporation, will act in the best interests of the Corporation and its stockholders and not in the interests of individual constituencies, and (f) intends to serve as a director for the full term for which such individual is to stand for election.

1.12.3 Special Meetings of Stockholders. Only such business shall be conducted at a special meeting of stockholders as shall have been brought before the meeting pursuant to the Corporation's notice of such meeting. Nominations of persons for election to the Board may be made at a special meeting of stockholders at which directors are to be elected pursuant to the Corporation's notice of such meeting (a) by or at the direction of the Board or any committee thereof or (b) provided that the Board has determined that directors shall be elected at such meeting, by any Record Stockholder at the time of giving of notice of the special meeting, who shall be entitled to vote at the meeting and who complies with the notice and other procedures set forth in this Section 1.12. In the event the Corporation calls a special meeting of stockholders for the purpose of electing one or more directors to the Board, any such Record Stockholder entitled to vote in the election of such directors may nominate a person or persons (as the case may be) for election to such position(s) as specified in the Corporation's notice of meeting, if the Record Stockholder's notice required by Section 1.12.1(b) is delivered to the Secretary of the Corporation at the principal executive offices of the Corporation (i) no earlier than the close of business on the one hundred twentieth (120th) day prior to such special meeting and (ii) no later than the close of business on the later of the ninetieth (90th) day prior to such special meeting or the tenth (10th) day following the day on which Public Announcement is first made of the date of the special meeting and of the nominees proposed by the Board to be elected at such meeting. In no event shall the adjournment or postponement of a special meeting commence a new time period (or extend any time period) for the giving of a Record Stockholder's notice as described above.

1.12.4 General.

a. Only such persons who are nominated in accordance with the procedures set forth in this Section 1.12 shall be eligible to be elected at a meeting of stockholders and to serve as directors and only such business shall be conducted at a meeting of stockholders as shall have been brought before the meeting in accordance with the procedures set forth in this Section 1.12. Except as otherwise provided by law, the chairperson of the meeting shall have the power and duty to determine whether a nomination or any other business proposed to be brought before the meeting was made or proposed, as the case may be, in accordance with the procedures set forth in this Section 1.12 and, if any proposed nomination or business was not made or proposed in compliance with this Section 1.12, to declare that such nomination shall be disregarded or that such proposed business shall not be transacted. Notwithstanding the foregoing provisions of this Section 1.12, unless otherwise required by law, if the stockholder (or a Qualified Representative (as defined below) of the stockholder) does not appear at the annual or special meeting of stockholders of the Corporation to present a nomination or proposed business, such nomination shall be disregarded and such proposed business shall not be transacted, notwithstanding that proxies in respect of such vote may have been received by the Corporation.
b. For purposes of these Bylaws, the following definitions shall apply:
    i. a person shall be deemed to be "***Acting in Concert***" with another person if such person knowingly acts (whether or not pursuant to an express agreement, arrangement or understanding) in concert with, or toward a common goal relating to the management, governance or control of the Corporation in substantial parallel with, such other person where (1) each person is conscious of the other person's conduct or intent and this awareness is an element in their decision-making processes and (2) at least one additional factor suggests that such persons intend to act in concert or in substantial parallel, which such additional factors

may include, without limitation, exchanging information (whether publicly or privately), attending meetings, conducting discussions or making or soliciting invitations to act in concert or in substantial parallel; provided that a person shall not be deemed to be Acting in Concert with any other person solely as a result of the solicitation or receipt of revocable proxies or consents from such other person in response to a solicitation made pursuant to, and in accordance with, Section 14(a) (or any successor provision) of the Exchange Act by way of a proxy or consent solicitation statement filed on Schedule 14A. A person Acting in Concert with another person shall be deemed to be Acting in Concert with any third party who is also Acting in Concert with such other person;

ii. "***affiliate***" and "***associate***" shall have the meanings ascribed thereto in Rule 405 under the Securities Act of 1933, as amended; provided, however, that the term "partner" as used in the definition of "associate" shall not include any limited partner that is not involved in the management of the relevant partnership;

iii. "***Associated Person***" shall mean with respect to any subject stockholder or other person (including any proposed nominee) (1) any person directly or indirectly controlling, controlled by or under common control with such stockholder or other person, (2) any beneficial owner of shares of stock of the Corporation owned of record or beneficially by such stockholder or other person, (3) any associate of such stockholder or other person, and (4) any person directly or indirectly controlling, controlled by or under common control or Acting in Concert with any such Associated Person;

iv. "***Compensation Arrangement***" shall mean any direct or indirect compensatory payment or other financial agreement, arrangement or understanding with any person or entity other than the Corporation, including any agreement, arrangement or understanding with respect to any direct or indirect compensation, reimbursement or indemnification in connection with candidacy, nomination, service or action as a nominee or as a director of the Corporation;

v. "***Competitor***" shall mean any entity that provides products or services that compete with or are alternatives to the principal products produced or services provided by the Corporation or its affiliates;

vi. "***Proposing Person***" shall mean (1) the Record Stockholder providing the notice of business proposed to be brought before an annual meeting or nomination of persons for election to the Board at a stockholder meeting, (2) the beneficial owner or beneficial owners, if different, on whose behalf the notice of business proposed to be brought before the annual meeting or nomination of persons for election to the Board at a stockholder meeting is made, and (3) any Associated Person on whose behalf the notice of business proposed to be brought before the annual meeting or nomination of persons for election to the Board at a stockholder meeting is made;

vii. "***Public Announcement***" shall mean disclosure in a press release reported by the Dow Jones News Service, Associated Press or comparable national news service or in a document publicly filed by the Corporation with the Securities and Exchange Commission pursuant to section 13, 14 or 15(d) of the Exchange Act; and

viii. to be considered a "***Qualified Representative***" of a stockholder, a person must be a duly authorized officer, manager, trustee or partner of such stockholder or must be authorized by a writing executed by such stockholder or an electronic transmission delivered by such stockholder to act for such stockholder as a proxy at the meeting of stockholders and such person must produce such writing or electronic transmission, or a reliable reproduction thereof, at the meeting. The Secretary of the Corporation, or any other person who shall be appointed to serve as secretary of the meeting, may require, on behalf of the Corporation, reasonable and appropriate documentation to verify the status of a person purporting to be a "Qualified Representative" for purposes hereof.

c. Notwithstanding the foregoing provisions of this Section 1.12, a stockholder shall also comply with all applicable requirements of the Exchange Act and the rules and regulations thereunder with respect to the matters set forth herein; provided however, that any references in these Bylaws to the Exchange Act or the rules and regulations promulgated thereunder are not intended to and shall not limit any requirements applicable to nominations or proposals as to any other business to be considered pursuant to this Section 1.12, and compliance with the requirements under this Section 1.12 shall be the exclusive means for a stockholder to make nominations or submit other business. Nothing in this Section 1.12 shall be deemed to affect any rights of (a) stockholders to request inclusion of proposals in the Corporation's proxy statement pursuant to Rule 14a-8 under the Exchange Act or (b) the holders of any series of Preferred Stock to elect directors elected by one or more series of Preferred Stock pursuant to any applicable provisions of the Certificate of Incorporation.

ARTICLE II: BOARD OF DIRECTORS

Section 2.1: Number; Qualifications. The number of directors constituting the Whole Board shall be the number fixed by, or determined in the manner provided in, the Certificate of Incorporation. No decrease in the authorized number of directors constituting the Whole Board shall shorten the term of any incumbent director. Directors need not be stockholders of the Corporation.

Section 2.2: Election; Resignation; Vacancies. Directors shall be elected for such terms and in the manner provided by the Certificate of Incorporation and applicable law. Each director shall hold office until such director's successor is duly elected and qualified, or until such director's earlier death, resignation or removal. Any director may resign at any time upon written notice to the Corporation. Such resignation shall be effective upon delivery unless it is specified to be effective at a later date or time or upon the occurrence of an event, in which case it shall be effective at such later date or time or upon the occurrence of such event. Except as otherwise provided by the Certificate of Incorporation or by applicable law, any vacancy in the Board resulting from the death, resignation, removal or disqualification of any director or for any other reason, and any newly created directorship resulting from any increase in the authorized number of directors to be elected by all stockholders entitled to vote generally in the election of directors, may be filled by the stockholders, by a majority of the directors then in office, even if less than a quorum, or by a sole remaining director.

Section 2.3: Regular Meetings. Regular meetings of the Board may be held at such place, within or without the State of Delaware, and at such times as the Board may from time to time determine. Notice of regular meetings need not be given if the date, times and places thereof are fixed by resolution of the Board.

Section 2.4: Special Meetings. Special meetings of the Board may be called by the Chairperson of the Board, the Lead Independent Director of the Board, the Chief Executive Officer, the President or a majority of the members of the Board then in office and may be held at any time, date or place, within or without the State of Delaware, as the person or persons calling the meeting shall fix. Notice of the time, date and place of such meeting shall be given orally (in person, by telephone or otherwise), in writing or by electronic transmission (including electronic mail), by the person or persons calling the meeting to all directors at least four (4) days before the meeting (if the notice is mailed) or at least twenty-four (24) hours before the meeting (if such notice is given orally, in person, by telephone or otherwise, or by hand delivery, or any means of electronic transmission, including electronic mail). Unless otherwise indicated in the notice, any and all business may be transacted at a special meeting.

Section 2.5: Remote Meetings Permitted. Members of the Board, or any committee of the Board, may participate in a meeting of the Board or such committee by means of conference telephone or other communications equipment by means of which all persons participating in the meeting can hear each other, and participation in a meeting pursuant to conference telephone or other communications equipment shall constitute presence in person at such meeting.

Section 2.6: Quorum; Vote Required for Action. Subject to Section 2.2 above, a majority of the Whole Board shall constitute a quorum for the transaction of business at any meeting of the Board. If a quorum shall fail to attend any meeting, a majority of those present may adjourn the meeting to another place, date or time without further notice thereof. Except as otherwise provided herein or in the Certificate of Incorporation, or required by law, the vote of a majority of the directors present at a meeting at which a quorum is present shall be the act of the Board.

Section 2.7: Organization. Meetings of the Board shall be presided over by the Chairperson of the Board or, in such person's absence, by the Chief Executive Officer or, in such person's absence, by the President or, in such person's absence, by a chairperson chosen by the Board at the meeting. The Secretary shall act as secretary of the meeting, but in such person's absence the chairperson of the meeting may appoint any person to act as secretary of the meeting.

Section 2.8: Action by Unanimous Consent of Directors. Any action required or permitted to be taken at any meeting of the Board, or of any committee thereof, may be taken without a meeting if all members of the Board or such committee, as the case may be, consent thereto in writing or by electronic transmission, and the writing or writings or electronic transmission or transmissions are filed with the minutes of proceedings of the Board or committee, respectively, in the minute books of the Corporation. Such filing shall be in paper form if the minutes are maintained in paper form and shall be in electronic form if the minutes are maintained in electronic form.

Section 2.9: Fees and Compensation of Directors. Unless otherwise restricted by the Certificate of Incorporation or these Bylaws, the Board shall have the authority to fix the compensation of directors, including without limitation compensation for services as members of committees of the Board. No such compensation shall preclude any director from serving the corporation in any other capacity and receiving compensation therefor.

Section 2.10: Chairperson of the Board. The Corporation may also have, at the discretion of the Board, a Chairperson of the Board who shall be elected from among its ranks and who shall have the power to preside at all meetings of the Board and have such other powers and duties as provided in these Bylaws and as the Board may from time to time prescribe. The Chairperson of the Board, as such, shall not be deemed to be an officer of the Corporation.

ARTICLE III: COMMITTEES

Section 3.1: Committees. The Board may designate one or more committees, each committee to consist of one or more of the directors of the Corporation. The Board may designate one or more directors as alternate members of any committee, who may replace any absent or disqualified member at any meeting of the committee. In the absence or disqualification of a member of the committee, the member or members thereof present at any meeting of such committee who are not disqualified from voting, whether or not such member or members constitute a quorum, may unanimously appoint another member of the Board to act at the meeting in place of any such absent or disqualified member. Any such committee, to the extent provided in a resolution of the Board, shall have and may exercise all the powers and authority of the Board in the management of the business and affairs of the Corporation and may authorize the seal of the Corporation to be affixed to all papers that may require it; but no such committee shall have the power or authority in reference to the following matters: (a) approving, adopting, or recommending to the stockholders any action or matter (other than the election or removal of members of the Board) expressly required by the DGCL to be submitted to stockholders for approval or (b) adopting, amending or repealing any bylaw of the Corporation.

Section 3.2: Committee Minutes; Committee Rules. Each committee shall keep regular minutes of its meetings and, except as otherwise provided in the resolutions of the Board establishing such committee, shall report the same to the Board as requested by the Board or as otherwise required. Unless the Board otherwise provides, each committee designated by the Board may make, alter and repeal rules for the conduct of its business. In the absence of such rules each committee shall conduct its business in the same manner as the Board conducts its business pursuant to Article II of these Bylaws.

ARTICLE IV: OFFICERS

Section 4.1: Generally. The officers of the Corporation shall consist of a Chief Executive Officer, a President, a Secretary and a Treasurer and may consist of such other officers, including a Chief Financial Officer, and one or more Vice Presidents, as may from time to time be appointed by the Board. All officers shall be elected by the Board; provided, however, that, notwithstanding anything to the contrary set forth herein, the Board may empower the Chief Executive Officer of the Corporation to appoint any officer other than the Chief Executive Officer, the President, the Chief Financial Officer or the Treasurer. Each officer shall hold office until such person's successor is appointed or until such person's earlier resignation, death or removal. Any number of offices may be held by the same person. Any officer may resign at any time upon written notice to the Corporation. Such resignation shall be effective upon delivery unless it is specified to be effective at a later date or time or upon the occurrence of an event, in which case it shall be effective at such later date or time or upon the occurrence of such event. Any vacancy occurring in any office of the Corporation by death, resignation, removal or otherwise may be filled by the Board or, if the vacancy is of an office that the Chief Executive Officer has been empowered to appoint, the Chief Executive Officer.

Section 4.2: Chief Executive Officer. Subject to the control of the Board and such supervisory powers, if any, as may be given by the Board, the powers and duties of the Chief Executive Officer of the Corporation are:

a. To act as the general manager and, subject to the control of the Board, to have general supervision, direction and control of the business and affairs of the Corporation;
b. Subject to Article I, Section 1.6 of these Bylaws, to preside at all meetings of the stockholders;
c. Subject to the Certificate of Incorporation and Article I, Section 1.2 of these Bylaws, to call special meetings of the stockholders to be held at such times and, subject to the limitations prescribed by law or by these Bylaws, at such places as he or she shall deem proper; and
d. To affix the signature of the Corporation to all deeds, conveyances, mortgages, guarantees, leases, obligations, bonds, certificates and other papers and instruments in writing which have been authorized by the Board or which, in the judgment of the Chief Executive Officer, should be executed on behalf of the Corporation; and, subject to the direction of the Board, to have general charge of the property of the Corporation and to supervise and control all officers, agents and employees of the Corporation.

Section 4.3: President. The person holding the office of Chief Executive Officer shall be the President of the Corporation unless the Board shall have designated one person as the President and a different person as the Chief Executive Officer of the Corporation. The President shall have all such powers and duties as are commonly incident to the office of President, including the power to sign certificates representing shares of capital stock of the Corporation, or that are delegated to him or her by the Board or the Chief Executive Officer (if such office is then held by a person other than the person holding the office of President). A President may be designated by the Board to perform the duties and exercise the powers of the Chief Executive Officer in the event of the Chief Executive Officer's absence or disability.

Section 4.4: Chief Operating Officer. The Chief Operating Officer shall have all such powers and duties as are commonly incident to the office of

Chief Operating Officer or that are delegated to him or her by the Board or the Chief Executive Officer. The Chief Operating Officer may be designated by the Board to perform the duties and exercise the powers of the Chief Executive Officer or President in the event of the Chief Executive Officer's or President's absence or disability.

Section 4.5: Vice President. Each Vice President shall have all such powers and duties as are commonly incident to the office of Vice President, including the power to sign certificates representing shares of capital stock of the Corporation, or that are delegated to him or her by the Board or the Chief Executive Officer. A Vice President may be designated by the Board to perform the duties and exercise the powers of the Chief Executive Officer or President in the event of the Chief Executive Officer's and President's absence or disability.

Section 4.6: Chief Financial Officer. The person holding the office of Chief Financial Officer shall be the Treasurer of the Corporation unless the Board shall have designated another officer as the Treasurer of the Corporation. Subject to the direction of the Board and the Chief Executive Officer, the Chief Financial Officer shall perform all duties and have all powers that are commonly incident to the office of Chief Financial Officer.

Section 4.7: Treasurer. The Treasurer shall have custody of all moneys and securities of the Corporation. The Treasurer shall make such disbursements of the funds of the Corporation as are authorized and shall render from time to time an account of all such transactions. The Treasurer shall also perform such other duties and have such other powers as are commonly incident to the office of Treasurer, including the power to sign certificates representing shares of capital stock of the Corporation, or as the Board or the Chief Executive Officer may from time to time prescribe.

Section 4.8: Secretary. The Secretary shall issue or cause to be issued all authorized notices for, and shall keep, or cause to be kept, minutes of all meetings of the stockholders and the Board. The Secretary shall have charge of the corporate minute books and similar records and shall perform such other duties and have such other powers as are commonly incident to the office of Secretary, including the power to sign certificates representing shares of capital stock of the Corporation, or as the Board or the Chief Executive Officer may from time to time prescribe.

Section 4.9: Delegation of Authority. The Board may from time to time delegate the powers or duties of any officer of the Corporation to any other officers or agents of the Corporation, notwithstanding any provision hereof.

Section 4.10: Removal. Any officer of the Corporation shall serve at the pleasure of the Board and may be removed at any time, with or without cause, by the Board; provided that if the Board has empowered the Chief Executive Officer to appoint any officer of the Corporation, then any such officer may be removed by the Chief Executive Officer. Such removal shall be without prejudice to the contractual rights of such officer, if any, with the Corporation.

Section 4.11: Representation of Shares of Other Corporations. Except as otherwise provided by the Board, and subject to the direction and control thereof, the Chief Executive Officer, the President, the Chief Operating Officer, any Vice President, the Chief Financial Officer, the Treasurer, the Secretary or any assistant secretary of this Corporation, or any other person authorized by the Board or the Chief Executive Officer, the Chief Operating Officer or the President or a Vice President, is authorized to vote, represent, and exercise on behalf of this Corporation all rights incident to any and all shares of any other corporation or corporations standing in the name of this Corporation. The authority granted herein may be exercised either by such person directly or by any other person authorized to do so by proxy or power of attorney duly executed by the person having such authority.

ARTICLE V: STOCK

Section 5.1: Certificates. The shares of capital stock of the Corporation shall be represented by certificates; provided, however, that the Board may provide by resolution or resolutions that some or all of any or all classes or series of its capital stock shall be uncertificated shares. Any such resolution shall not apply to shares represented by a certificate until such certificate is surrendered to the Corporation. Every holder of stock represented by certificates shall be entitled to have a certificate signed by, or in the name of the Corporation by, any two officers of the Corporation who are authorized to sign stock certificates representing the number of shares registered in certificate form. Each of the Chairperson of the Board, the Vice-Chairperson of the Board, the President, any Vice President, the Treasurer, any Assistant Treasurer, or the Secretary or any Assistant Secretary, of the Corporation shall be deemed to have the authority to sign stock certificates, representing the number of shares registered in certificate form. Any or all of the signatures on the certificate may be a facsimile. In case any officer, transfer agent or registrar who has signed or whose facsimile signature has been placed upon a certificate shall have ceased to be such officer, transfer agent or registrar before such certificate is issued, it may be issued by the Corporation with the same effect as if such person were an officer, transfer agent or registrar at the date of issue.

Section 5.2: Lost, Stolen or Destroyed Stock Certificates; Issuance of New Certificates or Uncertificated Shares. The Corporation may issue a new certificate of stock, or uncertificated shares, in the place of any certificate previously issued by it, alleged to have been lost, stolen or destroyed, upon the making of an affidavit of that fact by the person claiming the certificate of stock to be lost, stolen or destroyed, and the Corporation may require the owner of the certificate alleged to have been lost, stolen or destroyed, or such owner's legal representative, to give the Corporation a bond sufficient to indemnify it against any claim that may be made against it on account of the alleged loss, theft or destruction of any such certificate or the issuance of such new certificate or uncertificated shares.

Section 5.3: Other Regulations. The issue, transfer, conversion and registration of stock certificates and uncertificated shares shall be governed by such other regulations as the Board may establish.

ARTICLE VI: INDEMNIFICATION

Section 6.1: Indemnification of Officers and Directors. Each person who was or is made a party to, or is threatened to be made a party to, or is involved in any threatened, pending or completed action, suit or proceeding, whether civil, criminal, administrative, investigative, legislative or any other type whatsoever (a "**Proceeding**"), by reason of the fact that such person is or was a director or officer of the Corporation, or, while serving as a director or officer of the Corporation, is or was serving at the request of the Corporation as a director, officer, employee, agent or trustee of another corporation, or of a partnership, joint venture, trust or other enterprise, including service with respect to employee benefit plans (for purposes of this Article VI, an "**Indemnitee**"), shall be indemnified and held harmless by the Corporation to the fullest extent permitted by the DGCL, as the same exists or may hereafter be amended (but, in the case of such amendment, only to the extent that such amendment permits the Corporation to provide broader indemnification rights than such law permitted the Corporation to provide prior to such amendment), against all expenses, liability and loss (including attorneys' fees, judgments, fines, ERISA excise taxes and penalties and amounts paid in settlement) reasonably incurred or suffered by such Indemnitee in connection therewith, provided such Indemnitee acted in good faith and in a manner that the Indemnitee reasonably believed to be in or not opposed to the best interests of the Corporation, and, with respect to any criminal action or Proceeding, had no reasonable cause to believe the Indemnitee's conduct was unlawful. Such indemnification shall continue as to an Indemnitee who has ceased to be a director or officer of the Corporation and shall inure to the benefit of such Indemnitees' heirs, executors and administrators. Notwithstanding the foregoing, except as provided in Section 6.5, the Corporation shall not be obligated under this Article VI to indemnify any Indemnitee seeking indemnification in connection with a Proceeding (or part thereof) initiated by such Indemnitee unless such Proceeding (or part thereof) was authorized in the first instance by the Board.

Section 6.2: Advance of Expenses. The Corporation shall pay all expenses (including attorneys' fees) incurred by such an Indemnitee in defending any such Proceeding in advance of its final disposition; provided, however, that the payment of such expenses incurred by such an Indemnitee in advance of the final disposition of such Proceeding shall be made only upon delivery to the Corporation of an undertaking, by or on behalf of such Indemnitee, to repay all amounts so advanced if it shall ultimately be determined that such Indemnitee is not entitled to be indemnified under this Article VI or otherwise.

Section 6.3: Non-Exclusivity of Rights. The rights conferred on any person in this Article VI shall not be exclusive of any other right that such person may have or hereafter acquire under any statute, provision of the Certificate of Incorporation, Bylaw, agreement, vote or consent of stockholders or disinterested directors, or otherwise. Additionally, nothing in this Article VI shall limit the ability of the Corporation, in its discretion but subject to applicable law, to provide rights to indemnification or advancement of expenses to any person other than an Indemnified Person or to provide greater rights to indemnification and advancement of expenses than those provided in this Article VI to any Indemnified Person.

Section 6.4: Indemnification Agreements. The Board is authorized to cause the Corporation to enter into agreements with any director, officer, employee, agent or fiduciary of the Corporation, or any person serving at the request of the Corporation as a director, officer, employee, agent, fiduciary, trustee, partner or managing member of another corporation, partnership, limited liability company, joint venture, trust or other enterprise, including employee benefit plans, providing indemnification or advancement rights to such person. Such rights may be greater than those provided in this Article VI.

Section 6.5: Claims.

6.5.1 Right to Bring Suit. If a claim for indemnification (following the final disposition of such Proceeding) under Section 6.1 of this Article VI is not paid in full by the Corporation within sixty (60) days after a written claim has been received by the Corporation, or a claim for advancement of expenses is not paid in full within thirty (30) days after the Corporation has received a statement or statements therefor, the Indemnitee shall be entitled at any time thereafter (but not before) to bring suit against the Corporation to recover the unpaid amount of the claim. If successful in whole or in part in any such suit, or in a suit brought by the Corporation to recover an advancement of expenses pursuant to the terms of an undertaking, the Indemnitee shall be entitled, to the fullest extent permitted by law, to be paid also the expense of prosecuting or defending such suit. In (a) any suit brought by the Indemnitee to enforce a right to indemnification hereunder (but not in a suit brought by the Indemnitee to enforce a right to an advancement of expenses) it shall be a defense that, and (b) in any suit brought by the Corporation to recover an advancement of expenses pursuant to the terms of an undertaking, the Corporation shall be entitled to recover such expenses upon a final adjudication that, the Indemnitee has not met any applicable standard of conduct for entitlement to indemnification under applicable law.

6.5.2 Effect of Determination. Neither the failure of the Corporation (whether by its directors who are not parties to such action, a committee of such directors, independent legal counsel or its stockholders) to have made a determination prior to the commencement of a suit by the Indemnitee to enforce a right to indemnification that indemnification of the Indemnitee is proper in the circumstances because the Indemnitee has met the applicable standard of conduct to be entitled to indemnification under applicable law, nor an actual determination by the Corporation (whether by its directors who are not parties to such action, a committee of such directors, independent legal counsel or its stockholders) that the Indemnitee has not met such standard of conduct, shall create a presumption that the Indemnitee has not met such standard of conduct or, in the case of such a suit brought by the Indemnitee, be a defense to such suit.

6.5.3 Burden of Proof. In any suit brought by the Indemnitee to enforce a right to indemnification or to an advancement of expenses hereunder, or brought by the Corporation to recover an advancement of expenses pursuant to the terms of an undertaking provided hereunder, the burden of proving that the Indemnitee is not entitled to be indemnified, or is required to repay any amounts advanced pursuant to the terms of such undertaking, under this Article VI shall be on the Corporation.

Section 6.6: Nature of Rights. The rights conferred upon Indemnitees in this Article VI shall be contract rights and such rights shall continue as to an Indemnitee who has ceased to be a director, officer or trustee of the Corporation and shall inure to the benefit of the Indemnitee's heirs, executors and administrators. Any right to indemnification or to advancement of expenses arising under this Article VI shall not be eliminated or impaired by an amendment to these Bylaws after the occurrence of the act or omission that is the subject of the Proceeding for which indemnification or advancement of expenses is sought.

Section 6.7: Insurance. The Corporation may purchase and maintain insurance on behalf of any person who is or was a director, officer, employee, agent or fiduciary of the Corporation, or is or was serving at the request of the Corporation as a director, officer, employee, agent, fiduciary, trustee, partner or managing member of another corporation, partnership, limited liability company, joint venture, trust or other enterprise against any liability asserted against him or her and incurred by him or her in any such capacity, or arising out of his or her status as such, whether or not the Corporation would have the power to indemnify him or her against such liability under the provisions of the DGCL.

Section 6.8: Certain Defined Terms. Any reference to an officer of the Corporation in this Article VI shall be deemed to refer exclusively to the Chief Executive Officer, the President, the Chief Operating Officer, any Vice President, the Chief Financial Officer, the Treasurer or the Secretary appointed pursuant to Article IV of these Bylaws, and to any other officer of the Corporation appointed by (x) the Board pursuant to Article IV of these Bylaws or (y) an officer to whom the Board has delegated the power to appoint officers pursuant to Article IV of these Bylaws, and any reference to an officer of any other corporation, partnership, joint venture, trust, employee benefit plan or other enterprise shall be deemed to refer exclusively to an officer appointed by the board of directors (or equivalent governing body) of such other entity pursuant to the certificate of incorporation and bylaws (or equivalent organizational documents) of such other corporation, partnership, joint venture, trust, employee benefit plan or other enterprise. The fact that any person who is or was an employee of the Corporation or an employee of any other corporation, partnership, joint venture, trust, employee benefit plan or other enterprise has been given or has used the title of "vice president" or any other title that could be construed to suggest or imply that such person is or may be an officer of the Corporation or of such other corporation, partnership, joint venture, trust, employee benefit plan or other enterprise shall not result in such person being constituted as, or being deemed to be, an officer of the Corporation or of such other corporation, partnership, joint venture, trust, employee benefit plan or other enterprise for purposes of this Article VI.

ARTICLE VII: NOTICES

Section 7.1: Notice.
7.1.1 Form and Delivery. Except as otherwise specifically required in these Bylaws (including, without limitation, Section 2.4 above or Section 7.1.2 below) or by applicable law, all notices required to be given pursuant to these Bylaws shall be in writing and may (a) in every instance in connection with any delivery to a member of the Board, be effectively given by hand delivery (including use of a delivery service), by depositing such notice in the mail, postage prepaid, or by sending such notice by prepaid overnight express courier, facsimile, electronic mail or other form of electronic transmission and (b) be effectively be delivered to a stockholder when given by hand delivery, by depositing such notice in the mail, postage prepaid or by sending such notice by electronic transmission in accordance with the DGCL. Any such notice shall be addressed to the person to whom notice is to be given at such person's address as it appears on the records of the Corporation. Except as otherwise provided by law, the notice shall be deemed given (a) in the case of hand delivery, when received by the person to whom notice is to be given or by any person accepting such notice on behalf of such person, (b) in the case of delivery by mail, upon deposit in the mail, postage prepaid, (c) in the case of delivery by overnight express courier, when dispatched, and (d) in the case of delivery via electronic mail or other form of electronic transmission, when dispatched.

7.1.2 Electronic Transmission. Without limiting the manner by which notice otherwise may be given effectively to stockholders, any notice to stockholders given by the Corporation under any provision of the DGCL, the Certificate of Incorporation, or these Bylaws shall be effective if given by a form of electronic transmission in accordance with the DGCL.

7.1.3 Affidavit of Giving Notice. An affidavit of the Secretary or an Assistant Secretary or of the transfer agent or other agent of the Corporation that the notice has been given in writing or by a form of electronic transmission shall, in the absence of fraud, be prima facie evidence of the facts stated therein.

Section 7.2: Waiver of Notice. Whenever notice is required to be given under any provision of the DGCL, the Certificate of Incorporation or these Bylaws, a written waiver of notice, signed by the person entitled to notice, or waiver by electronic transmission by such person, whether before or after the time stated therein, shall be deemed equivalent to notice. Attendance of a person at a meeting shall constitute a waiver of notice of such meeting, except when the person attends a meeting for the express purpose of objecting at the beginning of the meeting to the transaction of any business because the meeting is not lawfully called or convened. Neither the business to be transacted at, nor the purpose of, any regular or special meeting of the stockholders, directors or members of a committee of directors need be specified in any waiver of notice.

ARTICLE VIII: MISCELLANEOUS

Section 8.1: Fiscal Year. The fiscal year of the Corporation shall be determined by resolution of the Board.

Section 8.2: Seal. The Board may provide for a corporate seal, which may have the name of the Corporation inscribed thereon and shall otherwise be in such form as may be approved from time to time by the Board.

Section 8.3: Form of Records. Any records administered by or on behalf of the Corporation in the regular course of its business, including its stock ledger, books of account, and minute books, may be kept on, or by means of, or be in the form of, any information storage device, method or one or more electronic networks or databases (including one or more distributed electronic networks or databases), provided that the records so kept can be converted into clearly legible paper form within a reasonable time. The Corporation shall so convert any records so kept upon the request of any person entitled to inspect such records pursuant to any provision of the DGCL.

Section 8.4: Severability. If any provision of these Bylaws shall be held to be invalid, illegal, unenforceable or in conflict with the provisions of the Certificate of Incorporation, then such provision shall, to the fullest extent permitted by law, be enforced to the maximum extent possible consistent with such holding and the remaining provisions of these Bylaws (including without limitation, all portions of any section of these Bylaws containing any such provision held to be invalid, illegal, unenforceable or in conflict with the Certificate of Incorporation, that are not themselves invalid, illegal, unenforceable or in conflict with the Certificate of Incorporation) shall remain in full force and effect.

ARTICLE IX: AMENDMENT

Notwithstanding any other provision of these Bylaws, any alteration, amendment or repeal of these Bylaws, or the adoption of new Bylaws, shall require the approval of the Board or the stockholders of the Corporation as provided by the Certificate of Incorporation and applicable law.

CERTIFICATION OF AMENDED AND RESTATED BYLAWS

OF

FACEBOOK, INC.

a Delaware corporation

I, David Kling, certify that I am Secretary of Facebook, Inc., a Delaware corporation (the "***Corporation***"), that I am duly authorized to make and deliver this certification, that the attached Bylaws are a true and complete copy of the Amended and Restated Bylaws of the Corporation in effect as of the date of this certificate.

Dated: April 10, 2019

/s/ David Kling

David Kling, Secretary

DOCUMENT FOUR

Notice of Annual Meeting and Proxy Statement (Facebook, Inc.)

DEFA14A 2016-04-15

https://www.sec.gov/Archives/edgar/data/1326801/000132680120000037/facebook2020definitive-prox.htm

DEF14A 1 facebook2020definitiveprox.htm

DEFINITIVE PROXY STATEMENT

UNITED STATES
SECURITIES AND EXCHANGE COMMISSION
Washington, D.C. 20549

SCHEDULE 14A INFORMATION

Proxy Statement Pursuant to Section 14(a) of the Securities Exchange Act of 1934
(Amendment No.)

Filed by the Registrant. ☒ Filed by a Party other than the Registrant. ☐

Check the appropriate box:

☐ Preliminary Proxy Statement
☐ Confidential, for Use of the Commission Only (as permitted by Rule 14a-6(e)(2))
☒ Definitive Proxy Statement
☐ Definitive Additional Materials
☐ Soliciting Material under § 240.14a-12

"Facebook Inc.'s Notice of 2020 Annual Shareholders' Meeting and Proxy Statement," https://www.sec.gov/Archives/edgar/data/1326801/000132680120000037/facebook2020definitiveprox.htm, U.S. Securities and Exchange Commission, 2016.

Facebook, Inc.

(Name of Registrant as Specified in Its Charter)
(Name of Person(s) Filing Proxy Statement if other than the Registrant)

Payment of Filing Fee (Check the appropriate box):

☒ No fee required.

☐ Fee computed on table below per Exchange Act Rules 14a-6(i)(1) and 0-11.

(1) Title of each class of securities to which transaction applies:

(2) Aggregate number of securities to which transaction applies:

(3) Per unit price or other underlying value of transaction computed pursuant to Exchange Act Rule 0-11 (Set forth the amount on which the filing fee is calculated and state how it was determined):

(4) Proposed maximum aggregate value of transaction:

(5) Total fee paid:

☐ Fee paid previously with preliminary materials.

☐ Check box if any part of the fee is offset as provided by Exchange Act Rule 0-11(a)(2) and identify the filing for which the offsetting fee was paid previously. Identify the previous filing by registration statement number, or the Form or Schedule and the date of its filing.

(1) Amount Previously Paid:

(2) Form, Schedule or Registration Statement No.:

(3) Filing Party:

(4) Date Filed:

FACEBOOK

1601 Willow Road
Menlo Park, California 94025

April 10, 2020

To Our Stockholders:

You are cordially invited to attend the 2020 Annual Meeting of Stockholders (Annual Meeting) of Facebook, Inc. to be held on May 27, 2020, at 10:00 a.m. Pacific Time. The Annual Meeting will be a completely virtual meeting of stockholders conducted via live audio webcast to enable our stockholders to participate from any location around the world that is convenient to them. You will be able to attend the Annual Meeting by visiting *www.virtualshareholdermeeting.com/FB2020.*

The matters expected to be acted upon at the Annual Meeting are described in detail in the accompanying Notice of Annual Meeting of Stockholders and proxy statement.

You may cast your vote over the Internet, by telephone, or by completing and mailing a proxy card to ensure that your shares will be represented. Your vote by proxy will ensure your representation at the Annual Meeting regardless of whether or not you attend. Returning the proxy does not deprive you of your right to attend and vote your shares electronically at the Annual Meeting.

Thank you for your continued investment in Facebook.

Mark Zuckerberg
Chairman and Chief Executive Officer

IMPORTANT NOTICE REGARDING THE AVAILABILITY OF PROXY MATERIALS FOR THE STOCKHOLDER MEETING TO BE HELD ON MAY 27, 2020: THIS PROXY STATEMENT AND THE ANNUAL REPORT ARE AVAILABLE AT www.proxyvote.com

Facebook, Inc.
1601 Willow Road
Menlo Park, California 94025

NOTICE OF ANNUAL MEETING OF STOCKHOLDERS
TO BE HELD ON MAY 27, 2020

To Our Stockholders:

NOTICE IS HEREBY GIVEN that the 2020 Annual Meeting of Stockholders (Annual Meeting) of Facebook, Inc. will be held on May 27, 2020, at 10:00 a.m. Pacific Time. The Annual Meeting will be a completely virtual meeting of stockholders conducted via live audio webcast. You will be able to attend the Annual Meeting by visiting *www.virtualshareholdermeeting.com/FB2020*.

We are holding the Annual Meeting for the following purposes, which are more fully described in the proxy statement accompanying this Notice:

1. To elect the following nine directors, all of whom are currently serving on our board of directors, each to serve until the next annual meeting of stockholders and until his or her successor has been elected and qualified, or until his or her earlier death, resignation, or removal:

   Peggy Alford
   Marc L. Andreessen
   Andrew W. Houston
   Nancy Killefer
   Robert M. Kimmitt
   Sheryl K. Sandberg
   Peter A. Thiel
   Tracey T. Travis
   Mark Zuckerberg

2. To ratify the appointment of Ernst & Young LLP as our independent registered public accounting firm for the fiscal year ending December 31, 2020.
3. To approve the director compensation policy.
4. To consider and vote upon eight stockholder proposals, if properly presented.

5. To transact such other business as may properly come before the Annual Meeting or any adjournment or postponement thereof.

The foregoing items of business are more fully described in the proxy statement accompanying this Notice.

Only stockholders of record at the close of business on April 3, 2020 are entitled to notice of, and to vote at, the Annual Meeting or any adjournment or postponement thereof. The Notice of Internet Availability of Proxy Materials (Notice), proxy statement and form of proxy are being distributed and made available on the Internet on or about April 10, 2020.

By Order of the Board of Directors,

David Kling
Vice President, Deputy General Counsel, and Secretary
Menlo Park, California

Whether or not you expect to attend the Annual Meeting, please vote at your earliest convenience by following the instructions in the Notice of Internet Availability of Proxy Materials or the proxy card you received in the mail.

TABLE OF CONTENTS

Facebook, Inc.

1601 Willow Road
Menlo Park, California 94025

PROXY STATEMENT

April 10, 2020

QUESTIONS AND ANSWERS ABOUT THE PROXY MATERIALS AND THE ANNUAL MEETING

1. **What are proxy materials?**

   The accompanying proxy is delivered and solicited on behalf of the board of directors of Facebook, Inc., a Delaware corporation, in connection with the 2020 Annual Meeting of Stockholders (Annual Meeting) to be held on May 27, 2020, at 10:00 a.m. Pacific Time, via live audio webcast in a virtual meeting format at *www.virtualshareholdermeeting.com/FB2020*. As a stockholder, you are invited to attend the Annual Meeting and are requested to vote on the items of business described in this proxy statement. This proxy statement includes information that we are required to provide to you under Securities and Exchange Commission (SEC) rules and is designed to assist you in voting your shares. The proxy materials include this proxy statement for the Annual Meeting, an annual report to stockholders, including our Annual Report on Form 10-K for the year ended December 31, 2019 (Annual Report), and the proxy card or a voting instruction form for the Annual Meeting (Proxy Materials).

2. **Why did I receive a notice in the mail regarding the Internet availability of proxy materials instead of a full set of proxy materials?**

   In accordance with the SEC rules, we may furnish proxy materials, including this proxy statement and our Annual Report, to our stockholders by providing access to such documents on the Internet instead of mailing printed copies. Accordingly, we are sending the Notice to our stockholders of record and beneficial stockholders as of April 3, 2020, which is the record date for the Annual Meeting.

3. **How can I access the proxy materials over the Internet?**

   The Notice and proxy card or voting instruction form included with the Proxy Materials will contain instructions on how to view the proxy materials on the Internet. Electronic copies of this proxy statement and the Annual Report are available at *www.proxyvote.com*.

4. **How can I sign up for the electronic proxy delivery service?**

   The Notice and proxy card or voting instruction form included with the Proxy Materials will contain instructions on how to request electronic delivery of future proxy materials. Choosing to receive your future proxy materials by email will eliminate the cost of printing and mailing documents and will reduce the associated environmental impact. If you choose to receive future proxy materials by email, you will receive an email next year with instructions containing a link to those materials and a link to the proxy voting site. Your election to receive proxy materials by email will remain in effect until you terminate it.

5. **I share an address with another stockholder. Why did we receive only one copy of the Proxy Materials and how may I obtain an additional copy of the Proxy Materials?**

   The SEC has adopted rules that permit companies and intermediaries (e.g., brokers) to satisfy the delivery requirements for the Proxy Materials or other annual meeting materials with respect to two or more stockholders sharing the same address by delivering a single set of Proxy Materials or other annual meeting materials addressed to those stockholders. This process, which is commonly referred to as "householding," is intended to provide extra convenience for stockholders and reduce costs.

   We and a number of brokers with account holders who are our stockholders will be householding our Proxy Materials. We will deliver a single set of Proxy Materials to multiple stockholders sharing an address unless contrary instructions have been received from the affected stockholders. Stockholders who participate in householding will continue to be able to access and receive separate proxy cards. If, at any time, you no longer wish to participate in householding and would prefer to receive a separate set of Proxy Materials, or if you are receiving multiple sets of Proxy Materials and would like to receive only one, please notify your broker, bank or other nominee if you are a beneficial stockholder or notify us if you are a registered stockholder. Registered stockholders can notify us by sending a written request to Facebook, Inc., c/o Broadridge Householding Department, 51 Mercedes Way, Edgewood, New York 11717, or by calling 1-866-540-7095, and we will promptly deliver any additional Proxy Materials requested.

6. **What items of business will be voted on at the Annual Meeting?**

   The items of business scheduled to be voted on at the Annual Meeting are:

- Proposal One: the election of nine directors;
- Proposal Two: the ratification of the appointment of Ernst & Young LLP as our independent registered public accounting firm for the fiscal year ending December 31, 2020;
- Proposal Three: the approval of the director compensation policy;
- Proposal Four: a stockholder proposal regarding change in stockholder voting;
- Proposal Five: a stockholder proposal regarding an independent chair;
- Proposal Six: a stockholder proposal regarding majority voting for directors;
- Proposal Seven: a stockholder proposal regarding political advertising;
- Proposal Eight: a stockholder proposal regarding human/civil rights expert on board;
- Proposal Nine: a stockholder proposal regarding report on civil and human rights risks;
- Proposal Ten: a stockholder proposal regarding child exploitation; and
- Proposal Eleven: a stockholder proposal regarding median gender/racial pay gap.

   The eight stockholder proposals (Proposals Four through Eleven) are hereinafter referred to as the "Stockholder Proposals." Other than the proposals described in this proxy statement, we are not aware of any other business to be acted upon at the Annual Meeting.

7. **How does the board of directors recommend I vote on these proposals?**

- "FOR" the election of each director nominee;
- "FOR" the ratification of the appointment of Ernst & Young LLP as our independent registered public accounting firm for the fiscal year ending December 31, 2020;
- "FOR" the approval of the director compensation policy; and
- "AGAINST" each of the eight Stockholder Proposals (Proposals Four through Eleven).

8. **Who is entitled to vote at the Annual Meeting?**

Only holders of record of our Class A common stock and Class B common stock at the close of business on April 3, 2020, which is the record date, will be entitled to vote at the Annual Meeting. At the close of business on April 3, 2020, we had 2,406,231,860 shares of Class A common stock outstanding and 444,551,440 shares of Class B common stock outstanding and entitled to vote. Holders of our Class A common stock are entitled to one vote for each share held as of the above record date. Holders of our Class B common stock are entitled to ten votes for each share held as of the above record date. Holders of our Class A common stock and Class B common stock will vote together as a single class on all matters described in this proxy statement.

A quorum is required for our stockholders to conduct business at the Annual Meeting. A quorum exists if stockholders holding at least a majority of the voting power of the shares of our Class A common stock and Class B common stock (voting together as a single class) entitled to vote are present at the Annual Meeting or represented by proxy.

Registered Stockholders. If your shares are registered directly in your name with our transfer agent, Computershare Trust Company, N.A. (Computershare), you are considered the stockholder of record with respect to those shares, and the Proxy Materials were provided to you directly by us. As the stockholder of record, you have the right to grant your voting proxy directly to the individuals listed on the proxy card or to vote at the Annual Meeting.

Beneficial Stockholders. If your shares are held in a stock brokerage account or by a bank or other nominee, you are considered the beneficial owner of shares held in "street name" and the Proxy Materials were forwarded to you by your broker, bank or other nominee, who is considered, with respect to those shares, the stockholder of record. As the beneficial owner, you have the right to direct your broker, bank or other nominee how to vote your shares. Beneficial owners are also invited to attend and vote at the Annual Meeting.

9. **What votes are required to approve each of the proposals?**

For Proposal One, directors will be elected by a plurality of the votes of the shares of our Class A common stock and Class B common stock (voting together as a single class) present or represented by proxy at the Annual Meeting and entitled to vote on the election of directors, which means that the nine nominees receiving the highest number of affirmative votes will be elected.

Approval of Proposals Two through Eleven requires the affirmative "FOR" vote of a majority of the votes of the shares of our Class A common stock and Class B common stock (voting together as a single class) properly cast "FOR" or "AGAINST" each such proposal.

10. **How are broker non-votes and abstentions counted?**

A broker non-vote occurs when shares held by a broker are not voted with respect to a particular proposal because the broker does not have discretionary authority to vote on the matter and has not received voting instructions from its clients. If your broker holds your shares in its name and you do not instruct your broker how to vote, your broker will only have discretion to vote your shares on "routine" matters. Where a proposal is not "routine," a broker who has not received instructions from its clients does not have discretion to vote its clients' uninstructed shares on that proposal. At our Annual Meeting, only the ratification of the appointment of our independent registered public accounting firm (Proposal Two) is considered a routine matter. All other proposals are considered "non-routine," and your broker will not have discretion to vote on these proposals.

Broker non-votes and abstentions by stockholders from voting (including brokers holding their clients' shares of record who cause abstentions to be recorded) will be counted towards determining whether or not a quorum is present. However, because broker non-votes and abstentions are not voted affirmatively or negatively, they will have no effect on the approval of any of the proposals.

11. **Why are we holding a virtual Annual Meeting?**

We are leveraging technology to hold a virtual Annual Meeting that expands convenient access to, and enables participation by, stockholders from any location around the world. We believe the virtual format encourages attendance and participation by a broader group of stockholders, while also reducing the costs and environmental impact associated with an in-person meeting. In addition, we also believe that it is appropriate given global health concerns associated with the COVID-19 pandemic. The virtual Annual Meeting will allow our stockholders to ask questions and to vote.

12. **How can I attend and participate in the Annual Meeting?**

The Annual Meeting will be a completely virtual meeting of stockholders conducted exclusively via live audio webcast. You will be able to attend the Annual Meeting by visiting *www.virtualshareholdermeeting.com/FB2020*. To participate in the Annual Meeting, you will need the 16-digit control number included on your Notice, proxy card, or voting instruction form. The Annual Meeting will begin promptly at 10:00 a.m. Pacific Time on May 27, 2020. We encourage you to access the virtual meeting website prior to the start time. Online check-in will begin at 9:45 a.m. Pacific Time, and you should allow ample time to ensure your ability to access the meeting.

We will hold our question and answer session with management immediately following the conclusion of the business to be conducted at the Annual Meeting. You may submit a question in advance of the meeting by visiting *www.proxyvote.com*.

You may submit a question at any time during the meeting by visiting *www.virtualshareholdermeeting.com/FB2020*. The Chairman of the meeting has broad authority to conduct the Annual Meeting in an orderly manner, including establishing rules of conduct. A copy of the rules of conduct will be available online at the Annual Meeting. A replay of the Annual Meeting will be available on our website at *http://investor.fb.com/* after the meeting.

13. **What if I have technical difficulties or trouble accessing the virtual meeting website during the check-in time or during the Annual Meeting?**

Technicians will be available to assist you if you experience technical difficulties accessing the virtual meeting website. If you encounter any difficulties accessing the virtual meeting during the check-in or meeting time, please call 800-586-1548 (domestic) or 303-562-9288 (international) for assistance.

14. **Can I vote at the Annual Meeting?**

You may vote your shares electronically at the Annual Meeting by using the control number on your Notice, proxy card, or voting instruction form and following the instructions at *www.virtualshareholdermeeting.com/FB2020*. If you have already voted previously by telephone or Internet, there is no need to vote again at the Annual Meeting unless you wish to revoke and change your vote.

15. **Can I vote by telephone or Internet?**

For beneficial stockholders with shares registered in the name of a brokerage firm or bank, a number of brokerage firms and banks are participating in a program that offers telephone and Internet voting options. Stockholders should refer to the voting instruction form provided by their brokerage firm or bank for instructions on the voting methods they offer. Registered stockholders with shares registered directly in their names with Computershare will also be able to vote by telephone and Internet. If your shares are held in an account at a brokerage firm or bank participating in this program or registered directly in your name with Computershare, you may vote those shares by calling the telephone number specified on your proxy or accessing the Internet website address specified on your proxy instead of completing and signing the proxy itself. Submitting a telephonic or Internet proxy will not affect your right to vote electronically at the Annual Meeting should you decide to attend the Annual Meeting. The telephone and Internet voting procedures are designed to authenticate stockholders' identities, to allow stockholders to give their voting instructions, and to confirm that stockholders' instructions have been recorded properly.

The accompanying proxy card provides instructions on how to vote via the Internet or by telephone.

16. **How will my proxy be voted?**

The proxy accompanying this proxy statement is solicited on behalf of our board of directors for use at the Annual Meeting. Stockholders are requested to vote via the Internet or by telephone, or, if you requested to receive printed proxy materials, by completing, dating, and signing the accompanying proxy and promptly returning it in the enclosed envelope. All signed, returned proxies that are not revoked will be voted in accordance with the instructions contained therein. Signed proxies that give no instructions as to how they should be voted on a particular proposal at the Annual Meeting will be voted in accordance with the recommendation of our board of directors set forth in this proxy statement: in the case of the election of directors, as a vote "FOR" the election of all nominees presented by the board of directors; in the case of the ratification of Ernst & Young LLP as our independent registered public accounting firm, as a vote "FOR" such ratification; in the case of the vote on the director compensation policy, as a vote "FOR" the approval of the policy; and in the case of each of the eight Stockholder Proposals, as a vote "AGAINST" each such proposal.

17. **How do I change or revoke my proxy?**

Any person signing a proxy in the form accompanying this proxy statement has the power to revoke it prior to the Annual Meeting or at the Annual Meeting prior to the vote pursuant to the proxy. A proxy may be revoked by a writing delivered to us stating that the proxy is revoked, by a subsequent proxy that is signed by the person who signed the earlier proxy and is delivered before or at the Annual Meeting, by voting again on a later date on the Internet or by telephone (only your latest Internet or telephone proxy submitted prior to the Annual Meeting will be counted), or by attendance at the Annual Meeting and voting electronically.

18. **Who will tabulate the votes?**

We have designated a representative of the Veaco Group as the Inspector of Elections who will tabulate the votes.

19. **Where can I find the voting results of the Annual Meeting?**

We will announce preliminary voting results at the Annual Meeting and publish final results on a Current Report on Form 8-K that we expect to file with the SEC within four business days after the Annual Meeting.

20. **How can I make proposals or make a nomination for director for next year's annual meeting?**

You may present proposals for action at a future meeting or submit nominations for election of directors only if you comply with the requirements of the rules established by the SEC and our amended and restated bylaws, as applicable.

In order for a stockholder proposal to be considered for inclusion in our proxy statement and form of proxy relating to our annual meeting of stockholders to be held in 2021, the proposal must be received by us at our principal executive offices no later than December 11, 2020.

Stockholders wishing to bring a proposal or nominate a director at the annual meeting to be held in 2021 (but not include it in our proxy materials) under our amended and restated bylaws must provide written notice of such proposal to our Secretary at our principal executive offices between close of business January 27, 2021 and close of business February 26, 2021 and comply with the other provisions of our amended and restated bylaws.

21. Who pays for the expenses of solicitation?

The expenses of soliciting proxies to be voted at the Annual Meeting will be paid by us. In addition to the mailing of the Proxy Materials and other soliciting materials, we or our directors, executive officers, employees, or agents may also solicit proxies in person, by telephone, or by electronic communication. Following the original mailing of the Proxy Materials and other soliciting materials, we will request that banks, brokers, custodians, nominees, and other record holders of our Class A common stock and Class B common stock forward copies of the Proxy Materials and other soliciting materials to persons for whom they hold shares of Class A common stock and Class B common stock and request authority for the exercise of proxies. We will reimburse banks, brokers, custodians, nominees, and other record holders for reasonable charges and expenses incurred in forwarding soliciting materials to their clients. Stockholders voting via the telephone or Internet should understand that there may be costs associated with telephonic or electronic access, such as usage charges from telephone companies and Internet service providers, which must be borne by the stockholder.

* * *

EXECUTIVE OFFICERS, DIRECTORS, AND CORPORATE GOVERNANCE

The following table provides information regarding our executive officers, directors, and director nominees as of April 10, 2020:

NAME	AGE	POSITION(S)
Mark Zuckerberg	35	Chairman and Chief Executive Officer
Sheryl K. Sandberg	50	Chief Operating Officer and Director
David M. Wehner	51	Chief Financial Officer
David B. Fischer	47	Chief Revenue Officer
Jennifer G. Newstead	50	Vice President and General Counsel
Mike Schroepfer	45	Chief Technology Officer
Peggy Alford(1)	48	Director
Marc L. Andreessen(1)(2)	48	Director
Kenneth I. Chenault(1)+	68	Director
Andrew W. Houston(2)	37	Director
Nancy Killefer	66	Director
Robert M. Kimmitt*	72	Director
Peter A. Thiel(2)	52	Director
Tracey T. Travis(1)	57	Director
Jeffrey D. Zients(1)+	53	Director

* Lead Independent Director
(1) Member of the audit & risk oversight committee
(2) Member of the compensation, nominating & governance committee
\+ Messrs. Chenault and Zients are not nominees for election at the Annual Meeting.

Mark Zuckerberg is our founder and has served as our Chief Executive Officer (CEO) and as a member of our board of directors since July 2004. Mr. Zuckerberg has served as Chairman of our board of directors since January 2012. Mr. Zuckerberg attended Harvard University where he studied computer science. We believe that Mr. Zuckerberg should serve as a member of our board of directors due to the perspective and experience he brings as our founder, Chairman, and CEO, and as our largest and controlling stockholder.

Sheryl K. Sandberg has served as our Chief Operating Officer (COO) since March 2008 and as a member of our board of directors since June 2012. From November 2001 to March 2008, Ms. Sandberg served in various positions at Google, Inc., most recently as Vice President, Global Online Sales & Operations. Ms. Sandberg also is a former Chief of Staff of the U.S. Department of the Treasury and previously served as a consultant with McKinsey & Company, a management consulting company, and as an economist with The World Bank. In addition to serving as our COO, Ms. Sandberg has been a member of the board of directors of SurveyMonkey (SVMK Inc.) since July 2015. Ms. Sandberg previously served as a member of the boards of directors of Starbucks Corporation from March 2009 to March 2012 and the Walt Disney Company from March 2010 to March 2018. Ms. Sandberg holds an A.B. in economics from Harvard University and an M.B.A. from Harvard Business School. We believe that Ms. Sandberg should serve as a member of our board of directors due to the perspective and experience she brings as our COO.

David M. Wehner has served as our Chief Financial Officer (CFO) since June 2014. Mr. Wehner joined us in November 2012 as our Vice President, Corporate Finance and Business Planning. From August 2010 until November 2012, Mr. Wehner served as Chief Financial Officer at Zynga Inc., a provider of social game services. From February 2001 to July 2010, Mr. Wehner served in various positions at Allen & Company, an investment bank, including as a Managing Director from November 2006 to July 2010 and as a director from December 2005 to November 2006. In addition to serving as our CFO, Mr. Wehner has served on the board of directors of Alector, Inc., a clinical-stage biotechnology company, since October 2018. Mr. Wehner holds a B.S. in chemistry from Georgetown University and an M.S. in applied physics from Stanford University.

David B. Fischer has served in various positions with us since April 2010, most recently as our Chief Revenue Officer. Mr. Fischer previously served as our Vice President, Business and Marketing Partnerships from February 2012 to March 2019. From July 2002 to March 2010, Mr. Fischer served in various positions at Google, including most recently as its Vice President,

Global Online Sales & Operations. Prior to joining Google, Mr. Fischer served as Deputy Chief of Staff of the U.S. Department of the Treasury and was an associate editor at the U.S. News & World Report, L.P., a news magazine company. Mr. Fischer holds a B.A. in government from Cornell University and an M.B.A. from the Stanford University Graduate School of Business.

Jennifer G. Newstead has served as our Vice President and General Counsel since June 2019. From January 2018 to April 2019, Ms. Newstead served as the Legal Adviser of the U.S. Department of State. From July 2006 to January 2018, Ms. Newstead was a partner with the law firm of Davis Polk & Wardwell LLP. Ms. Newstead previously served in senior government positions as General Counsel of the Office of Management and Budget from 2003 to 2005, Special Assistant to the President and Associate White House Counsel from 2002 to 2003, and Principal Deputy Assistant Attorney General of the Office of Legal Policy at the U.S. Department of Justice from 2001 to 2002. Ms. Newstead previously served as a law clerk for Justice Stephen Breyer of the United States Supreme Court and Judge Laurence Silberman of the U.S. Court of Appeals for the D.C. Circuit, and as an Adjunct Professor of Law at Georgetown University Law Center. Ms. Newstead holds an A.B. in government from Harvard University and a J.D. from Yale Law School.

Mike Schroepfer has served in various positions with us since September 2008, most recently as our Chief Technology Officer (CTO). From December 2005 to August 2008, Mr. Schroepfer served as Vice President of Engineering at Mozilla Corporation, an Internet company. Prior to Mozilla, Mr. Schroepfer served in various positions at Sun Microsystems, Inc., an information technology company, including as Chief Technology Officer of its data center automation division. He also co-founded CenterRun, Inc., a developer of application provisioning software, which was acquired by Sun Microsystems. In addition to serving as our CTO, Mr. Schroepfer previously served as a member of the board of directors of Ancestry.com Inc. from January 2011 to December 2012. Mr. Schroepfer holds a B.S. and an M.S. in computer science from Stanford University.

Peggy Alford has served as a member of our board of directors since May 2019. Ms. Alford has served as Executive Vice President, Global Sales of PayPal Holdings, Inc., a digital payments company, since March 2020, and previously served as Senior Vice President, Core Markets from March 2019 to March 2020. From September 2017 to February 2019, Ms. Alford served as Chief Financial Officer and Head of Operations for the Chan Zuckerberg Initiative, a philanthropic organization. Ms. Alford previously held a variety of senior positions at PayPal from

May 2011 to August 2017, including Vice President, Chief Financial Officer of Americas, Global Customer and Global Credit, and Senior Vice President of Human Resources, People Operations and Global Head of Cross Border Trade. From 2007 to 2011, Ms. Alford served as President and General Manager of Rent.com, an eBay Inc. company, and also served as its Chief Financial Officer from October 2005 to March 2009. From 2002 to 2005, Ms. Alford served as Marketplace Controller and Director of Accounting Policy at eBay. Ms. Alford has served on the board of directors of the Macerich Company, a real estate investment trust, since June 2018. Ms. Alford holds a B.S. in accounting and business administration from the University of Dayton. We believe that Ms. Alford should serve as a member of our board of directors due to her extensive leadership and business experience, as well as her experience with finance and product development.

Marc L. Andreessen has served as a member of our board of directors since June 2008. Mr. Andreessen is a co-founder and has been a General Partner of Andreessen Horowitz, a venture capital firm, since July 2009. Previously, Mr. Andreessen co-founded and served as the Chairman of the board of directors of Opsware, Inc. (formerly known as Loudcloud Inc.), a software company. He also served as Chief Technology Officer of America Online, Inc., an Internet services company. Mr. Andreessen was a co-founder of Netscape Communications Corporation, a software company, serving in various positions, including Chief Technology Officer and Executive Vice President of Products. In addition to serving on our board of directors, Mr. Andreessen currently serves as a member of the boards of directors of several private companies. Mr. Andreessen previously served as a member of the boards of directors of eBay Inc. from September 2008 to October 2014, Hewlett-Packard Company from September 2009 to October 2015, and Hewlett Packard Enterprise Company from November 2015 to April 2018. Mr. Andreessen holds a B.S. in computer science from the University of Illinois at Urbana-Champaign. We believe that Mr. Andreessen should serve as a member of our board of directors due to his extensive leadership and business experience as an Internet entrepreneur, venture capitalist, and technologist, as well as his service on other boards of directors.

Kenneth I. Chenault has served as a member of our board of directors since February 2018. Mr. Chenault has served as Chairman and a Managing Director of General Catalyst, a venture capital firm, since February 2018. Mr. Chenault previously served as Chief Executive Officer of American Express Company, a financial services company, from January 2001 to February 2018, and as Chairman of American Express Company from April 2001 to

February 2018. Mr. Chenault joined American Express in 1981 as Director of Strategic Planning and served subsequently in a number of increasingly senior positions, including Vice Chairman and President and Chief Operating Officer, until his appointment as Chief Executive Officer. Mr. Chenault also previously served on the boards of directors of International Business Machines Corporation from October 1998 to February 2019 and The Procter & Gamble Company from April 2008 to February 2019. Mr. Chenault holds a B.A. in history from Bowdoin College and a J.D. from Harvard Law School. Mr. Chenault's term as a member of our board of directors will end at the Annual Meeting, and we thank him for his distinguished service.

Andrew W. Houston has served as a member of our board of directors since February 2020. Mr. Houston has served as Chief Executive Officer and Chairman of the board of directors of Dropbox, Inc., a global collaboration platform, since June 2007. Mr. Houston holds a B.S. in electrical engineering and computer science from the Massachusetts Institute of Technology. We believe that Mr. Houston should serve as a member of our board of directors due to his extensive leadership, entrepreneurship, and business experience as chief executive officer of a large technology company, as well as his experience with product innovation and development.

Nancy Killefer has served as a member of our board of directors since March 2020. Ms. Killefer served as a Senior Partner at McKinsey & Company, an international management consulting firm, from 1992 until her retirement in August 2013. Ms. Killefer joined McKinsey in 1979 and held a number of leadership roles, including serving as a member of the firm›s governing board. Ms. Killefer also served as Assistant Secretary for Management, Chief Financial Officer, and Chief Operating Officer of the U.S. Department of the Treasury from 1997 to 2000 and as a member of the IRS Oversight Board from 2000 to 2005, including as Chair of the IRS Oversight Board from 2002 to 2004. Ms. Killefer has served on the boards of directors of Cardinal Health, Inc., a healthcare services company, since September 2015, Taubman Centers, Inc., a real estate investment trust, since January 2019, and Natura & Company, a global personal care cosmetics group, since January 2020. Ms. Killefer also previously served on the boards of directors of Computer Sciences Corporation from August 2013 to November 2015, the Advisory Board Company from September 2013 to November 2017, CSRA, Inc. from November 2015 to April 2018, and Avon Products, Inc. from September 2013 to January 2020. Ms. Killefer holds a B.A. in economics from Vassar College and an M.S. in management from the Massachusetts Institute of Technology. We believe that Ms. Killefer should serve as a member of our board of directors due to her extensive leadership experience in both the public and private sector, as well as her finance experience and service on other boards of directors.

Robert M. Kimmitt has served as a member of our board of directors and as our Lead Independent Director since March 2020. Ambassador Kimmitt has served as Senior International Counsel at Wilmer Cutler Pickering Hale and Dorr LLP, an international law firm, since April 2009. From 2005 to 2009, Ambassador Kimmitt served as Deputy Secretary of the U.S. Department of the Treasury. From 2001 to 2005, he served as Executive Vice President of Global Public Policy at Time Warner, a media and entertainment company. From 2000 to 2001, Ambassador Kimmitt served as Vice Chairman and President of Commerce One, a software company. From 1997 to 2000, Ambassador Kimmitt was a partner at Wilmer Cutler & Pickering. Previously, Ambassador Kimmitt served as managing director at Lehman Brothers from 1993 to 1997, United States Ambassador to Germany from 1991 to 1993, Under Secretary of State for Political Affairs from 1989 to 1991, partner at Sidley & Austin LLP from 1987 to 1989, General Counsel for the U.S. Department of the Treasury from 1985 to 1987, and National Security Council Executive Secretary and General Counsel from 1983 to 1985. Ambassador Kimmitt has extensive public company board experience, most recently serving as a member of the supervisory board of Deutsche Lufthansa AG from April 2010 to May 2018. Ambassador Kimmitt holds a B.S. from the United States Military Academy at West Point and a J.D. from Georgetown University Law Center. Ambassador Kimmitt is a decorated combat veteran of the Vietnam War and attained the rank of Major General in the U.S. Army Reserve. We believe that Ambassador Kimmitt should serve as a member of our board of directors due to his distinguished public service and experience with legal, regulatory, and public policy issues, as well as his extensive private sector leadership and finance experience, including service on other boards of directors.

Peter A. Thiel has served as a member of our board of directors since April 2005. Mr. Thiel has served as President of Thiel Capital, an investment firm, since 2011 and a Partner of Founders Fund, a venture capital firm, since 2005. In 1998, Mr. Thiel co-founded PayPal, Inc., an online payment company, where he served as Chief Executive Officer, President, and Chairman of its board of directors from 2000 until its acquisition by eBay in 2002. Mr. Thiel holds a B.A. in philosophy from Stanford University and a J.D. from Stanford Law School. We believe that Mr. Thiel should serve as a member of our board of directors due to his extensive leadership and business experience as an entrepreneur and venture capitalist, as well as his role as one of our early investors and longest-serving directors. Mr. Thiel also has experience with technology and product innovation, and service on other boards of directors.

Tracey T. Travis has served as a member of our board of directors since March 2020. Ms. Travis has served as Executive Vice President and Chief Financial Officer of The Estée Lauder Companies Inc., a global manufacturer and marketer of skin care, makeup, fragrance, and hair care products, since August 2012. From January 2005 to July 2012, Ms. Travis served as Senior Vice President and Chief Financial Officer of Ralph Lauren Corporation, a luxury and apparel company. Ms. Travis previously served as Senior Vice President of Finance of Limited Brands from 2002 to 2004 and Chief Financial Officer of Intimate Brands Inc. from 2001 to 2002. From 1999 to 2001, Ms. Travis served as Chief Financial Officer of the Americas Group of American National Can. From 1989 to 1999, Ms. Travis held various management positions at PepsiCo/Pepsi Bottling Group. Ms. Travis began her career at General Motors Co. as an engineer and senior financial analyst. Ms. Travis has served on the board of directors of Accenture plc, a professional services company, since July 2017 and previously served on the board of directors of Campbell Soup Company from November 2011 to November 2017. Ms. Travis holds a B.S.E. in industrial engineering from the University of Pittsburgh and an M.B.A. in finance and operations from Columbia University. We believe that Ms. Travis should serve as a member of our board of directors due to her extensive leadership and business experience, as well as her experience with finance and consumer products.

Jeffrey D. Zients has served as a member of our board of directors since May 2018. Mr. Zients has served as CEO of the Cranemere Group Limited, a diversified holding company, since January 2018 and has served as President and a member of its board of directors since September 2017. Mr. Zients served in the Obama Administration from 2009 to 2017, including as Director of the National Economic Council for President Obama and Acting Director of the Office of Management and Budget. He also founded and managed Portfolio Logic LLC, an investment firm, from 2003 to 2009. From 1992 to 2004, Mr. Zients served in various roles at the Advisory Board Company, a research and consulting firm, including as Chairman from 2001 to 2004 and Chief Executive Officer from 1998 to 2000. He also served as Chairman of the Corporate Executive Board, a business research firm, from 2000 to 2001. Mr. Zients holds a B.A. in political science from Duke University. Mr. Zients' term as a member of our board of directors will end at the Annual Meeting, and we thank him for his distinguished service.

Executive Officers

Our executive officers are designated by, and serve at the discretion of, our board of directors. There are no family relationships among any of our directors or executive officers.

Board of Directors

Our board of directors may establish the authorized number of directors from time to time by resolution. The current authorized number of directors is 11. Each of our director nominees, if elected, will serve as a director until the next annual meeting of stockholders and until his or her successor has been elected and qualified, or until his or her earlier death, resignation, or removal.

Our board of directors held 13 meetings during 2019. In 2019, no incumbent member of our board of directors attended fewer than 75% of the aggregate of (i) the total number of meetings of the board of directors (held during the period for which he or she was a director) and (ii) the total number of meetings held by all committees of the board of directors on which such director served (held during the period that such director served). Members of our board of directors are invited and encouraged to attend each annual meeting of stockholders. Five directors attended our 2019 Annual Meeting of Stockholders.

Generally, each regular meeting of our board of directors includes an executive session of our independent directors without management present. Executive sessions also may be held at other times as needed. As more fully described below, our Lead Independent Director presides at executive sessions of the independent directors.

Board Leadership Structure

We believe that our current board structure is effective in supporting strong board leadership. The board of directors does not require the separation of the offices of Chair and CEO. However, when the positions of Chair and CEO are held by the same person, as is currently the case with Mr. Zuckerberg, our corporate governance guidelines provide that the independent directors shall designate a Lead Independent Director. Susan D. Desmond-Hellmann served as our Lead Independent Director from 2015 to 2019, and our independent directors designated Ambassador Kimmitt to serve as Lead Independent Director upon his appointment to our board of directors in March 2020.

As Chairman of our board of directors, Mr. Zuckerberg presides over meetings of the board of directors and may call special meetings of the board of directors. Mr. Zuckerberg brings valuable insight to our board of directors due to the perspective and experience he brings as our founder and CEO. As a result of his leadership since our inception, Mr. Zuckerberg has unparalleled knowledge of our business, products, and operations. As our largest and controlling stockholder, Mr. Zuckerberg is invested in our long-term success.

As our Lead Independent Director, Ambassador Kimmitt provides independent oversight and promotes effective communication between our board of directors and management, including Mr. Zuckerberg. Our Lead Independent Director is appointed annually to serve until his or her successor has been appointed and qualified, or until his or her earlier death, resignation, or removal, or such time as he or she is no longer an independent director. As more fully described in our corporate governance guidelines, our Lead Independent Director role includes the following authority and responsibilities, among others:

- presiding at all meetings of the board of directors at which the Chairman is not present, including executive sessions of the independent directors;
- calling separate meetings of the independent directors or special meetings of the full board of directors;
- facilitating discussion and open dialogue among the independent directors during meetings of the board of directors, executive sessions, and otherwise;
- serving as principal liaison between the independent directors and the Chairman;
- providing the Chairman with feedback and counsel concerning his interactions with the board of directors;
- providing leadership to the board of directors if circumstances arise in which the role of the Chairman may be, or may be perceived to be, in conflict;
- coordinating with the Chairman to set the agenda for meetings of the board of directors, taking into account input from other independent directors; and
- leading our board of directors in governance matters in coordination with our compensation, nominating & governance committee, including the evaluation of the performance of the CEO, the selection of committee chairs and memberships, and our annual board of directors and committee self-evaluations.

Our Lead Independent Director also performs such additional duties as the board of directors may otherwise determine and delegate.

Controlled Company Status

Because Mr. Zuckerberg controls a majority of our outstanding voting power, we are a "controlled company" under the corporate governance rules of The Nasdaq Stock Market LLC (Nasdaq). Therefore, we are not required to have a majority of our board of directors be independent, nor are we required to have a compensation committee or an independent nominating function. We have nevertheless opted to have a majority of our board of directors be independent and to have a compensation, nominating & governance committee comprised of independent directors, as more fully described below.

Director Independence

The rules of Nasdaq generally require that a majority of the members of a listed company's board of directors be independent. In addition, the Nasdaq rules generally require that, subject to specified exceptions, each member of a listed company's audit, compensation, and governance committees be independent. Although we are a "controlled company" under the corporate governance rules of Nasdaq and, therefore, are not required to comply with certain rules requiring director independence, we have nevertheless opted, under our corporate governance guidelines, to have a majority of the members of our board of directors be independent.

Audit & risk oversight committee members must also satisfy the independence criteria set forth in Rule 10A-3 under the Securities Exchange Act of 1934, as amended (Exchange Act). In order to be considered independent for purposes of Rule 10A-3, a member of an audit committee of a listed company may not, other than in his or her capacity as a member of the audit committee, the board of directors, or any other board committee: accept, directly or indirectly, any consulting, advisory, or other compensatory fee from the listed company or any of its subsidiaries; or be an affiliated person of the listed company or any of its subsidiaries.

Our board of directors has determined that none of our current non-employee directors has a relationship that would interfere with the exercise of independent judgment in carrying out the responsibilities of a director and that each of these directors is "independent" as that term is defined under the rules of Nasdaq. In addition, our board of directors determined that Erskine B. Bowles, Susan D. Desmond-Hellmann, and Reed Hastings were each independent during the time that they served as directors in 2019.

Our board of directors has also determined that Messrs. Andreessen, Chenault, and Zients and Mses. Alford and Travis, who comprise our audit & risk oversight committee, and Messrs. Andreessen, Houston, and Thiel, who comprise our compensation, nominating & governance committee, satisfy the respective independence standards for those committees established by applicable SEC rules and Nasdaq rules. With respect to the independence of Ms. Alford, Mr. Andreessen, Mr. Houston, and Ms. Travis, our board of directors considered that PayPal Holdings, Inc. (PayPal), of which Ms. Alford is Executive Vice President, Global Sales, OfferUp, Inc., of which Mr. Andreessen may be deemed a significant stockholder in 2019, Dropbox, Inc. (Dropbox), of which Mr. Houston is Chief Executive Officer and Chairman of the board of directors, and The Estée Lauder Companies Inc., of which Ms. Travis is Executive Vice President and Chief Financial Officer, purchased and in some cases received credits to purchase advertising from us in the ordinary course of business pursuant to our standard terms and conditions, including through a competitive bid auction. Our board of directors also considered that we made payments to PayPal and Dropbox for services relating to payment processing and data storage, respectively, in the ordinary course of business pursuant to standard terms and conditions. With regard to Ms. Alford, Mr. Andreessen, Mr. Houston, and Ms. Travis, our board of directors determined that such arrangements, transactions, or relationships do not interfere with the exercise of independent judgment by these directors in carrying out their responsibilities as our directors.

Additionally with respect to Ms. Alford, our board of directors considered that she served as Chief Financial Officer and Head of Operations for the Chan Zuckerberg Initiative for approximately 18 months prior to joining our board of directors. Our board of directors determined that this prior affiliation with the Chan Zuckerberg Initiative does not interfere with Ms. Alford's exercise of independent judgment in carrying out her responsibilities as a director based on the short term of her service to such organization and her conduct as a director over the past year.

In addition, our board of directors considered that Ambassador Kimmitt is senior international counsel at the law firm of Wilmer Cutler Pickering Hale and Dorr LLP (WilmerHale), an international law firm based in Washington, D.C. From time to time and in the ordinary course of its business, WilmerHale provides legal services to Facebook that we consider to be immaterial to their overall business. Ambassador Kimmitt has only provided de minimis legal services to Facebook over the past three years and will not provide any such services during his term as a director. Ambassador Kimmitt is not an equity partner in the firm and does not receive any compensation from the firm that is generated by or related to our payments to WilmerHale for such services. In addition, WilmerHale has agreed to implement certain measures to help ensure that Ambassador Kimmitt is walled off from any legal representation of Facebook undertaken by WilmerHale. Further, our compensation, nominating & governance committee reviewed the nature of Facebook's engagement of WilmerHale and the services rendered, including the expertise and relevant experience of the firm and the specific partners engaged to work on the matters for which we have engaged the firm, and determined that Ambassador Kimmitt's service on our board should not impair our company's ability to engage WilmerHale when our company determines such engagements to be appropriate and in our best interests. Our compensation, nominating & governance committee is satisfied that WilmerHale, when engaged for legal work, is chosen by our company's legal group on the basis of the directly relevant factors of experience, expertise, and efficiency. After taking into account all relevant facts and circumstances, our board of directors determined that Facebook's professional engagement of WilmerHale does not interfere with Ambassador Kimmitt's exercise of independent judgment in carrying out his responsibilities as a director.

Classified Board

So long as the outstanding shares of our Class B common stock represent a majority of the combined voting power of our outstanding common stock, we will not have a classified board of directors, and all directors will be elected for annual terms. As of the close of business on April 3, 2020, the outstanding shares of our Class B common stock represented a majority of the combined voting power of our outstanding common stock.

However, our restated certificate of incorporation and our amended and restated bylaws provide that when the outstanding shares of our Class B common stock represent less than a majority of the combined voting power of our outstanding common stock, we will have a classified board of directors consisting of three classes of approximately equal size, each serving staggered three-year terms. At such time, our directors will be assigned by the then-current board of directors to a class. Upon expiration of the term of a class of directors, directors for that class will be elected for three-year terms at the annual meeting of stockholders in the year in which that term expires. As a result, only one class of directors will be elected at each annual meeting of our stockholders, with the other classes continuing for the remainder of their respective three-year terms. Each director's term continues until the next annual meeting of stockholders and until his or her successor has been elected and qualified, or until his or her earlier death, resignation, or removal.

In addition, when the outstanding shares of our Class B common stock represent less than a majority of the combined voting power of our outstanding common stock and we have a classified board, only our board of directors may fill vacancies on our board. Any additional directorships resulting from an increase in the number of directors will be distributed among the three classes so that, as nearly as possible, each class will consist of one-third of the total number of directors.

The classification of our board of directors, if implemented, may have the effect of delaying or preventing changes in our control or management.

Board Committees

Our board of directors has established an audit & risk oversight committee and a compensation, nominating & governance committee, each of which has the composition and responsibilities described below. Members serve on these committees until their resignations or until otherwise determined by our board of directors. Our board of directors has adopted a written charter for each of these committees, which are available on our website at *http://investor.fb.com/governance.cfm*.

In addition, our board of directors plans to establish a standing privacy committee comprised of independent directors to oversee our obligations under the modified consent order we entered into in July 2019 with the U.S. Federal Trade Commission (FTC), which is pending federal court approval and which, among other matters, will require us to implement a comprehensive expansion of our privacy program.

From time to time, the board of directors may also establish ad hoc committees to address particular matters. For example, in April 2019, our board of directors established a special committee of independent directors to oversee the process involving the inquiry by the FTC into our compliance with our existing FTC consent order. Following our July 2019 settlement and entry into a modified FTC consent order, which is pending federal court approval, this special committee continued to oversee our efforts to prepare for implementation of the requirements of the modified consent order. This special committee was comprised of Messrs. Andreessen, Chenault, and Zients and held 13 meetings in 2019.

The following table provides information regarding the current composition of our standing committees:

DIRECTOR	AUDIT & RISK OVERSIGHT COMMITTEE(1)	COMPENSATION, NOMINATING & GOVERNANCE COMMITTEE(2)(3)
Peggy Alford	*	
Marc L. Andreessen	*	*
Kenneth I. Chenault(4)	*	
Andrew W. Houston		*
Nancy Killefer		
Robert M. Kimmitt		
Sheryl K. Sandberg		
Peter A. Thiel		+
Tracey T. Travis	*	
Jeffrey D. Zients(4)	+	
Mark Zuckerberg		

* Committee member
\+ Committee chair

(1) In 2019, Erskine B. Bowles also served on our audit & risk oversight committee until May 2019. Tracey T. Travis and Peggy Alford were appointed to our audit & risk oversight committee in March 2020 and April 2020, respectively. Following the Annual Meeting, Ms. Travis will serve as chair of our audit & risk oversight committee.
(2) In October 2019, our board of directors amended the charter of our compensation & governance committee to incorporate certain additional nominating functions and re-named the committee as the compensation, nominating & governance committee. We will not distinguish between the prior and current committee name and will refer to the compensation, nominating & governance committee throughout this proxy statement.
(3) In 2019, the chair of our compensation, nominating & governance committee was Reed Hastings from January until May, Susan D. Desmond-Hellmann from May until October, and Peter A. Thiel from October through the end of 2019. Andrew W. Houston was appointed to our compensation, nominating & governance committee in April 2020.
(4) Messrs. Chenault and Zients are not nominees for election at the Annual Meeting and their terms as directors will end at the Annual Meeting. We thank Messrs. Chenault and Zients for their distinguished service.

Audit & Risk Oversight Committee

As more fully described in its charter, our audit & risk oversight committee is directly responsible for, among other things:

- selecting the independent registered public accounting firm to audit our financial statements;
- ensuring the independence of the independent registered public accounting firm;
- discussing the scope and results of the audit with the independent registered public accounting firm, and reviewing, with management and that firm, our interim and year-end operating results;
- developing procedures to enable submission of anonymous concerns about accounting or auditing matters;
- considering the adequacy of our internal accounting controls and audit procedures;
- reviewing related party transactions;
- reviewing our program for promoting and monitoring compliance with applicable legal and regulatory requirements;

- overseeing our major risk exposures and the steps management has taken to monitor and control such exposures, and assisting our board of directors in overseeing the risk management of our company;
- pre-approving all audit and non-audit services to be performed by the independent registered public accounting firm; and
- overseeing our internal audit function.

Our audit & risk oversight committee is currently comprised of Messrs. Andreessen, Chenault, and Zients and Mses. Alford and Travis. Mr. Zients is the chair of our audit & risk oversight committee. Messrs. Chenault and Zients are not nominees for election at the Annual Meeting. Following the Annual Meeting, Ms. Travis will serve as chair of our audit & risk oversight committee. Each of our audit & risk oversight committee members qualifies as an audit committee financial expert, as that term is defined under SEC rules, and possesses financial sophistication as defined under the rules of Nasdaq. The designation does not impose on such directors any duties, obligations or liabilities that are greater than are generally imposed on members of our audit & risk oversight committee and our board of directors.

During 2019, the audit & risk oversight committee met in person, by telephone, or by videoconference ten times.

Compensation, Nominating & Governance Committee

As more fully described in its charter, our compensation, nominating & governance committee is responsible for, among other things:

- evaluating the performance of our executive officers;
- evaluating, recommending, approving and reviewing executive officer compensation arrangements, plans, policies and programs maintained by us;
- administering our equity-based compensation plans and our annual bonus plan;
- considering and making recommendations regarding non-employee director compensation;
- considering and making recommendations to our board of directors regarding its remaining responsibilities relating to executive compensation;
- reviewing and developing policies regarding the desired knowledge, experience, skills, diversity, and other characteristics of members of our board of directors and its committees, as well as our director nomination and committee appointment processes;

- identifying, evaluating, and recommending potential candidates for nomination to and membership on our board of directors and certain of its committees;
- monitoring succession planning for certain of our key executives;
- developing and recommending corporate governance guidelines and policies;
- overseeing the annual self-evaluation process for our board of directors and committees thereof;
- reviewing and granting proposed waivers of the code of conduct for executive officers; and
- advising our board of directors on corporate governance matters and board of director performance matters, including recommendations regarding the size, structure, and composition of our board of directors and committees thereof.

Our compensation, nominating & governance committee is currently comprised of Messrs. Andreessen, Houston, and Thiel. Mr. Thiel is the chair of our compensation, nominating & governance committee. Each member of this committee is a non-employee director, as defined pursuant to Rule 16b-3 promulgated under the Exchange Act.

During 2019, the compensation, nominating & governance committee met in person, by telephone, or by videoconference 11 times.

The charter for our compensation, nominating & governance committee allows the committee from time to time to delegate its authority to subcommittees and to our officers, as it may be deemed necessary or appropriate. In December 2013, our compensation committee (which was a predecessor to our compensation, nominating & governance committee) authorized the formation and delegation of certain authority to an equity subcommittee, which is now a subcommittee of the compensation, nominating & governance committee. The current members of the equity subcommittee are Ms. Sandberg and Mr. Wehner, and the members, acting either individually or jointly, have the authority to review and approve grants of restricted stock units (RSUs) to employees and consultants, other than to directors and our executive officers, which are reviewed and approved by our compensation, nominating & governance committee. The compensation, nominating & governance committee has not adopted a written charter for the equity subcommittee.

Privacy Committee

Our board of directors intends to establish a privacy committee following the effectiveness of our modified FTC consent order, which committee will be responsible for overseeing our comprehensive privacy program to be adopted in compliance with the order, among other things.

Policy Regarding Nominations

The policy of our board of directors is to encourage the selection of directors who will contribute to Facebook's success and our mission to give people the power to build community and bring the world closer together. Our compensation, nominating & governance committee is responsible for identifying and evaluating candidates for membership on our board of directors, based on the criteria set forth in our corporate governance guidelines, and has sole authority to recommend nominees to our board of directors. The compensation, nominating & governance committee considers recommendations from other directors, stockholders, management, and others as it deems appropriate and uses the same criteria for evaluating candidates regardless of the source of the recommendation. Our board of directors is responsible for nominating persons for election to our board of directors upon the recommendation of our compensation, nominating & governance committee.

Facebook is committed to a policy of inclusiveness and to pursuing diversity in terms of background and perspective. As such, when evaluating candidates for nomination as new directors, it is the policy of our compensation, nominating & governance committee to consider candidates with diverse backgrounds in terms of knowledge, experience, skills, and other characteristics, and to ensure that the initial list of candidates from which new director nominees are chosen by the board includes candidates with a diversity of race, ethnicity, and gender. In evaluating potential candidates for nomination, our compensation, nominating & governance committee considers the foregoing in light of the specific needs of the board of directors at that time. In addition, our compensation, nominating & governance committee considers director tenure in connection with evaluating current directors for nomination for re-election.

Stockholders who would like to recommend director candidates for consideration by our compensation, nominating & governance committee should send a notice of proposal to our Secretary at our principal executive offices. Stockholders desiring to nominate a director candidate at the annual meeting must comply with certain other procedures. We explain the procedures for nominating a director candidate at next year's annual meeting in the section entitled "Questions and Answers About the Proxy Materials and the Annual Meeting—How can I make proposals or make a nomination for director for next year's annual meeting?"

Board Performance and Composition

Our board of directors and its committees conduct an annual self-assessment of the performance of the board of directors, each committee, and each director. Our compensation, nominating & governance committee, in coordination with our Lead Independent Director, oversees the self-assessment process, and the results are reported to the board of directors. Our compensation, nominating & governance committee and our board of directors also periodically review the composition of the board of directors to ensure that it appropriately reflects the knowledge, experience, skills, diversity, and other characteristics required to fulfill its duties.

Our board of directors believes that its composition appropriately reflects the knowledge, experience, skills, diversity, and other characteristics required to fulfill its duties. The current director nominees have diverse backgrounds and perspectives that enable them to provide valuable guidance on both strategic and operational issues. All of our nominees have extensive leadership and compliance experience, as well as corporate governance expertise arising from service on other boards of directors. Many of our nominees have global business experience, including through service as CEO or in other senior corporate leadership positions involving management of complex operations, business challenges, risks, and growth. Several nominees have experience with technology or product innovation and development, entrepreneurship, and the dynamics of our industry. Other nominees have served in government positions and gained experience with significant regulatory and public policy issues. Our nominees also have a demonstrated sense of social mission, having contributed to social causes through nonprofit organizations and/or philanthropy. Our board of directors benefits from these qualifications, as well as the perspectives of nominees with in-depth knowledge of our company through their service as executive officers.

Our board of directors also believes that the current director nominees represent an effective balance with respect to director tenure. Ms. Alford joined the board of directors in 2019, and Mr. Houston, Mses. Killefer and Travis, and Ambassador Kimmitt joined the board of directors in 2020. These additions provide our board of directors with fresh perspectives and diverse experiences, while directors with longer tenure provide continuity and valuable insight into our business and strategy. The following table provides information regarding the tenure of our nominees for election at the Annual Meeting:

Tenure on Board of Directors	**Number of Director Nominees**
More than 10 years	3
6-10 years	1
0-5 years	5

Director Orientation and Education

We provide a number of onboarding sessions for new members of our board of directors to engage with our management team and learn more about our company priorities, strategy, and operations, as well as key issues and risks facing our industry, business, and community. Our management team also regularly engages with our directors throughout the year to provide updates across these areas, including in-depth reviews of relevant issues from subject matter experts.

Board Role in Risk Oversight

Our board of directors as a whole has responsibility for overseeing our risk management and believes that a thorough and strategic approach to risk oversight is critical. The board of directors exercises this oversight responsibility directly and through its committees. The oversight responsibility of the board of directors and its committees is informed by regular reports from our management team, including senior personnel that lead a variety of functions across the business, and from our internal audit department, as well as input from external advisors, as appropriate. These reports are designed to provide timely visibility to the board of directors and its committees about the identification and assessment of key risks, our risk mitigation strategies, and ongoing developments.

The full board of directors has primary responsibility for evaluating strategic and operational risk management, and for CEO succession planning. Our audit & risk oversight committee has responsibility for overseeing certain of our major risk exposures, including in the areas of financial and enterprise risk, legal and regulatory compliance, privacy and data use, community safety and security, and cybersecurity, as well as risks in other areas as our audit & risk oversight committee deems necessary or appropriate from time to time. Our audit & risk oversight committee also oversees the steps we have taken to monitor or mitigate these exposures, including policies and procedures for assessing and managing risk and related compliance efforts. Our board of directors also may exercise direct oversight with respect to these areas or delegate such oversight to committees in its discretion. For example, the special committee of the board formed in connection with our negotiations with the FTC assisted in oversight of the implementation of the requirements of the consent order we entered into with the FTC, including the oversight of certain risks related to privacy and data use. In addition, our audit & risk oversight committee oversees our internal audit function. Our compensation, nominating & governance committee evaluates risks arising from our corporate governance and compensation policies and practices, as more fully described in the section of this proxy statement entitled "Executive

Compensation—Compensation Discussion and Analysis—Compensation Risk Assessment," and oversees succession planning for certain key executives other than the CEO. Each of these committees provide reports to the full board of directors regarding these and other matters.

Compensation, Nominating & Governance Committee Interlocks and Insider Participation

During 2019, Dr. Desmond-Hellmann and Messrs. Andreessen, Hastings, and Thiel served on our compensation, nominating & governance committee. None of them has at any time in the last fiscal year been one of our officers or employees and Dr. Desmond-Hellmann and Mr. Hastings have since retired from our board of directors. Moreover, none of our executive officers has served as a member of the board of directors, or as a member of the compensation or similar committee, of any entity that has one or more executive officers who served on our board of directors or compensation, nominating & governance committee during 2019.

Director Compensation

Non-Employee Director Compensation Arrangements

In 2019, each non-employee member of our board of directors received an annual retainer fee of $50,000. In addition, members of our audit & risk oversight committee (other than the chair) received an annual retainer fee of $20,000, and the chair of our audit & risk oversight committee received an annual retainer fee of $50,000. Our Lead Independent Director received an additional annual retainer fee of $50,000. Each of these cash retainers is paid on a quarterly basis in advance of service for each quarter.

Each of our non-employee directors who is a sitting member of our board of directors as of the date of our annual meeting of stockholders for each such year (including directors who join the board of directors on the date of such annual meeting) also is eligible to receive an annual grant of RSUs equal to $300,000 divided by the average daily closing price of our Class A common stock in May of such year. These awards are approved each year automatically on the later of June 1 or the date of our annual meeting of stockholders for the particular year. These awards will vest fully on the earlier of (i) May 15 of the following year or (ii) the date of our annual meeting of stockholders of the following year if the director does not stand for re-election or is not re-elected at such annual meeting, so long as the recipient is a director on such date.

In 2019, following our annual meeting of stockholders, an annual grant of 1,613 RSUs was made to each non-employee director, which was equal to $300,000 divided by the average daily closing price of our Class A common stock in May 2019, which was $186.08 per share. The grant date for each award was June 17, 2019. These RSUs vest on May 15, 2020, so long as the non-employee director is a member of our board of directors on such date.

New non-employee directors who join our board of directors between our annual meetings of stockholders are eligible to receive a grant of RSUs at the time of their appointment with a value equal to the value of our annual grant of RSUs to our non-employee directors, prorated for service from the date of their appointment through the first following occurrence of May 15. Similarly, annual cash retainers for new non-employee directors are prorated during a director's first year of service.

On an annual basis, our compensation, nominating & governance committee reviews and makes recommendations to our board of directors regarding our non-employee director compensation arrangements, and our board of directors reviews and approves non-employee director compensation. As part of this review, our compensation, nominating & governance committee considers our directors' responsibilities and time commitments, as well as information regarding director compensation paid at peer companies, including an evaluation by its independent compensation consultant, Compensia, Inc.

In February 2020, based on the recommendation of our compensation, nominating & governance committee, our board of directors determined that certain changes should be made to our non-employee director compensation arrangements in order to fairly compensate our directors for the heavy workload, the increase in the number of board and committee meetings, the external scrutiny faced by our non-employee directors, the addition of our to-be-formed privacy committee, and the need to provide suitable compensation for the non-employee directors serving in leadership roles. Our compensation, nominating & governance committee considered Compensia's review of peer group and other market data, as well as Compensia's determination that the proposed changes were reasonable and justifiable based on the objectives of our non-employee director compensation program, the relative projected scale of workload and risk, and relevant market and peer data. Considering Compensia's findings and in light of other factors facing our non-employee directors, our board of directors determined that it is in the best interests of us and our stockholders to have our stockholders approve the proposed changes to our non-employee director compensation arrangements. The proposed changes to our non-employee director compensation arrangements are further described in "Proposal Three: Approval of the Director Compensation Policy."

2019 Director Compensation

The following table presents the total compensation for each person who served as a non-employee member of our board of directors during 2019. Other than as set forth in the table and described more fully below, in 2019 we did not pay any fees to, make any equity awards to, or pay any other compensation to the non-employee members of our board of directors who served as members during 2019. Mr. Zuckerberg and Ms. Sandberg do not receive compensation for their service as directors. Total compensation for Mr. Zuckerberg and Ms. Sandberg for their service as employees during 2019 is presented in "Executive Compensation—2019 Summary Compensation Table" below. See "Proposal Three: Approval of the Director Compensation Policy" for a discussion of proposed changes to compensation payable to certain of our non-employee directors in 2020 and going forward.

DIRECTOR NAME	FEES EARNED OR PAID IN CASH ($)	STOCK AWARDS ($)[1]	TOTAL ($)
Peggy Alford[2]	29,444	304,873	334,317
Marc L. Andreessen[3]	70,000	304,873	374,873
Erskine B. Bowles[4]	29,167	—	29,167
Kenneth I. Chenault[5]	70,000	304,873	374,873
Susan D. Desmond-Hellmann[6]	92,500	304,873	397,373
Reed Hastings[7]	20,833	—	20,833
Peter A. Thiel[8]	50,000	304,873	354,873
Jeffrey D. Zients[9]	100,000	304,873	404,873

(1) Amounts reflect the aggregate grant date fair value of the RSUs, computed in accordance with Financial Accounting Standards Board ASC Topic 718 (ASC 718). This amount does not reflect the actual economic value realized by the director.
(2) As of December 31, 2019, Ms. Alford held 1,613 RSUs, which will vest on May 15, 2020 so long as Ms. Alford is a member of our board of directors on such date.
(3) As of December 31, 2019, Mr. Andreessen held 1,613 RSUs, which will vest on May 15, 2020 so long as Mr. Andreessen is a member of our board of directors on such date.
(4) Mr. Bowles served on our board of directors until our annual meeting of stockholders in May 2019.
(5) As of December 31, 2019, Mr. Chenault held 1,613 RSUs, which will vest on May 15, 2020 so long as Mr. Chenault is a member of our board of directors on such date.
(6) Dr. Desmond-Hellmann served on our board of directors until October 2019. Dr. Desmond-Hellmann held 1,613 RSUs on the date of her resignation from our board of directors, which were canceled on such date without having vested.
(7) Mr. Hastings served on our board of directors until our annual meeting of stockholders in May 2019.
(8) As of December 31, 2019, Mr. Thiel held 1,613 RSUs, which will vest on May 15, 2020 so long as Mr. Thiel is a member of our board of directors on such date.
(9) As of December 31, 2019, Mr. Zients held 1,613 RSUs, which will vest on May 15, 2020 so long as Mr. Zients is a member of our board of directors on such date.

Mr. Houston was appointed to our board of directors in February 2020, and Mses. Killefer and Travis and Ambassador Kimmitt were appointed to our board of directors in March 2020. In connection with their appointments and in accordance with our existing compensation arrangements for non-employee directors, our board of directors approved the prorated grants of 391 RSUs to Mr. Houston, 270 RSUs to each of Mses. Killefer and Travis, and 203 RSUs to Ambassador Kimmitt as compensation for their service as members of our board of directors. These RSUs were granted on February 18, 2020 for Mr. Houston and on March 16, 2020 for Mses. Killefer and Travis, and will be granted on April 15, 2020 for Ambassador Kimmitt. These RSUs will vest in full on May 15, 2020, subject to continued service as a director through such date. In addition, Mr. Houston, Mses. Killefer and Travis, and Ambassador Kimmitt each will receive an annual retainer fee of $50,000, which will be prorated for service during 2020. Ms. Travis will receive an additional retainer of $20,000 in connection with her service on our audit & risk oversight committee until the Annual Meeting, which will increase to $50,000 upon her appointment as chair of our audit & risk oversight committee following the Annual Meeting, and Ambassador Kimmitt will receive an additional retainer of $150,000 in connection with his service as Lead Independent Director, each of which will be prorated for service during 2020. Mr. Houston, Mses. Killefer and Travis, and Ambassador Kimmitt will also be eligible for the proposed changes to our non-employee director compensation arrangements as described in "Proposal Three: Approval of the Director Compensation Policy," including, if the proposal is approved by our stockholders, the $1,000,000 equity grant for non-employee directors appointed starting in 2020, which vests in sixteen equal quarterly installments over a period of approximately four years.

Stock Ownership Guidelines and Transactions in Our Securities

Our directors are also subject to stock ownership guidelines and certain prohibitions on transactions in our securities. For more information, see "Executive Compensation—Compensation Discussion and Analysis—Stock Ownership Guidelines and Transactions in Our Securities."

Executive Compensation

Compensation Discussion and Analysis

Overview

This section explains our executive compensation philosophy, objectives, and design; our compensation governance; our compensation-setting process; our executive compensation program elements; and the decisions made in 2019 with respect to the compensation of each of our named executive officers. Our named executive officers for 2019, who appear in the section entitled "—2019 Summary Compensation Table" below, are:

- Mark Zuckerberg, our founder, Chairman, and Chief Executive Officer (CEO);
- Sheryl K. Sandberg, our Chief Operating Officer (COO);
- David M. Wehner, our Chief Financial Officer (CFO);
- Mike Schroepfer, our Chief Technology Officer (CTO); and
- Jennifer G. Newstead, our Vice President and General Counsel (GC).

Executive Compensation Philosophy, Objectives, and Design

Philosophy. We are focused on our mission to give people the power to build community and bring the world closer together. We believe that we are still in the early stages of this journey and that for us to be successful we must hire and retain a talented team of engineering, product, sales, and general and administrative professionals who can help achieve this mission through the successful pursuit of our company priorities. In addition, we expect our executive team to possess and demonstrate strong leadership and management capabilities. For more information regarding our 2019 company priorities, see the section entitled "—Elements of Executive Compensation" below.

Objectives. Our compensation program for our named executive officers is built to support the following objectives:

- attract the top talent in our leadership positions and motivate our executives to deliver the highest level of individual and team impact and results;
- encourage our executives to focus on our company priorities;
- ensure each of our executives receives a total compensation package that encourages his or her longterm retention;
- reward high levels of performance with commensurate levels of compensation; and
- align the interests of our executives with those of our stockholders in the overall success of our company by emphasizing long-term incentives.

Design. Our executive compensation program continues to be heavily weighted towards equity compensation, in the form of restricted stock units (RSUs), with cash compensation that is generally below market relative to executive compensation at our peer companies. We believe that equity compensation offers the best vehicle to focus our executive officers on our mission and the successful pursuit of our company priorities, and to align their interests with the long-term interests of our stockholders.

We typically grant our executive officers an annual equity award with service-based vesting conditions where the commencement of vesting is deferred until a future date, as discussed further in the section entitled "—Elements of Executive Compensation—Equity Compensation" below. When combined with the executives' prior equity awards, we believe that these additional awards represent a strong long-term retention tool and provide the executive officers with effective long-term equity incentives.

Our compensation, nominating & governance committee evaluates our executive compensation program, including our mix of cash and equity compensation, on an annual basis or as circumstances require based on our business objectives and the competitive environment for talent. For the near future, we anticipate continuing our emphasis on pay-for-performance and delivering the substantial majority of compensation in RSUs that vest over a minimum of four years.

Compensation Governance

The compensation, nominating & governance committee seeks to ensure sound executive compensation practices to adhere to our pay-for-performance philosophy while appropriately managing risk and aligning our executive compensation program with long-term stockholder interests. The following principles were the guiding factors of our pay-for-performance practices during 2019:

- the compensation, nominating & governance committee is comprised solely of independent directors;
- the compensation, nominating & governance committee conducts an annual review and approval of our compensation strategy with assistance from its independent compensation consultant, Compensia, Inc. (Compensia), a national compensation consulting firm, including a review of our compensation-related risk profile to ensure that our compensation-related risks are not reasonably likely to have a material adverse effect on our company;
- the compensation, nominating & governance committee retains discretion on bonus payouts to enable it to respond to unforeseen events and adjust bonus payouts, as appropriate;

- we do not offer post-employment payments or benefits, other than certain death-related benefits that are generally available to all employees; and
- our compensation philosophy and related governance features are complemented by several specific policies and practices that are designed to align our executive compensation program with long-term stockholder interests, including the following:
- our executives are subject to company-wide policies that prohibit trading in futures and derivative securities and engaging in hedging activities relating to our securities, holding our securities in margin accounts, pledging our securities as collateral for loans, and engaging in short sales of our securities;
- our executives are subject to stock ownership guidelines that require them to maintain significant ownership of our common stock;
- we offer limited perquisites that are for business-related purposes or necessary for the security of our executive officers; and
- our executives participate in broad-based company-sponsored health and welfare benefits programs on the same basis as our other full-time, salaried employees.

Compensation-Setting Process

Role of Our Compensation, Nominating & Governance Committee. The compensation, nominating & governance committee is responsible for overseeing all aspects of our executive compensation program, including executive salaries, payouts under our bonus plan, the size and structure of equity awards, and any executive perquisites. The compensation, nominating & governance committee is solely responsible for determining the compensation of our CEO and reviews and approves the compensation of our other executive officers. For more information regarding the responsibilities of the compensation, nominating & governance committee, see the section entitled "Executive Officers, Directors, and Corporate Governance—Board Committees."

Role of Management. In setting compensation for 2019, our CEO, our COO, and our Head of People provided their views to the compensation, nominating & governance committee on how to implement our compensation philosophy through our executive compensation program and attended meetings of the compensation, nominating & governance committee. Our CEO and COO made recommendations to the compensation, nominating & governance committee regarding compensation for our executive officers other than for themselves because of their daily involvement with our executive team. No executive officer participated directly in the final deliberations or determinations regarding his or her own compensation package or was present during such determinations, except for our CEO who has requested that his base salary be fixed at $1 per year.

Our management team and the compensation, nominating & governance committee each play a role in evaluating and mitigating any risk that may exist relating to our compensation plans, practices, and policies for all employees, including our named executive officers, as further described in the section entitled "—Compensation Risk Assessment" below.

Role of Compensation Consultant. The compensation, nominating & governance committee has the authority to engage its own advisors to assist in carrying out its responsibilities. In 2019, the compensation, nominating & governance committee engaged the services of Compensia to advise the committee regarding the amount and types of compensation that we provide to our executives and how our compensation practices compared to the compensation practices of other companies. Compensia is engaged directly by the compensation, nominating & governance committee. Compensia does not provide any services to us other than the services provided to the compensation, nominating & governance committee. The compensation, nominating & governance committee has reviewed, and will continue to review going forward, the independence of Compensia under applicable SEC and Nasdaq rules and believes that Compensia does not have any conflicts of interest in advising the committee.

Use of Comparative Market Data. We aim to compensate our executive officers at levels that are commensurate with the most competitive levels of compensation for executives in similar positions at the group of publicly-traded peer companies set forth below, with whom we compete for hiring and retaining executive talent (our Peer Group). In making compensation decisions, the compensation, nominating & governance committee also considers the scope of responsibility of each executive officer, our current practice of maintaining minimal differentiation between the cash compensation packages of our executive officers, the unvested balances of equity awards held by each executive officer, as well as the compensation, nominating & governance committee's assessment of each executive officer's performance and impact on the organization. In determining 2019 compensation, the compensation, nominating & governance committee did not use a formula for taking into account these different factors.

We analyze market data for executive compensation at least annually using the most relevant published survey sources, information available from public filings, and input from Compensia. Management and

Compensia provided the compensation, nominating & governance committee with both cash and equity compensation data for our Peer Group, which was selected from companies that meet some or all of the criteria listed below:

- technology or media company;
- key talent competitor;
- minimum revenue of $10 billion; and/or
- minimum market capitalization of $50 billion.

In the second quarter of 2018, using this criteria as a baseline, the compensation, nominating & governance committee approved the following companies for inclusion in our Peer Group for 2019:

Alphabet	Microsoft
Amazon.com	Netflix
Apple	PayPal Holdings
AT&T	salesforce.com
CBS	The Walt Disney Company
Cisco Systems	Twenty-First Century Fox
Comcast	Verizon Communications

In December 2018, the compensation, nominating & governance committee reviewed our executive compensation against this Peer Group to ensure that our executive officer compensation was competitive and sufficient to recruit and retain our executive officers. Compensia provided the compensation, nominating & governance committee with an analysis of total cash compensation data (base salaries and cash bonus awards at target) and total direct compensation data (total cash compensation and equity compensation) at various percentiles. While the compensation, nominating & governance committee considered this data in determining executive officer compensation, we did not seek to benchmark our executive compensation to any pre-set "target" percentile of the competitive market. Rather, the compensation, nominating & governance committee sought to compensate our executive officers at a level that would allow us to successfully recruit and retain the best possible talent for our executive team. Compensia's analysis did not include our GC who joined our company in June 2019. Our compensation, nominating & governance committee subsequently considered comparative Peer Group and other market data provided by Compensia when determining our GC's 2019 compensation.

Further, as our revenue and market capitalization have increased significantly over the last several years, the compensation, nominating & governance committee gives greater weight to the compensation levels of companies in our Peer Group that have higher revenue and market capitalization compared to other companies in the Peer Group when making decisions about the compensation of our executive officers. The compensation, nominating & governance committee also relies on the knowledge and experience of its members and our management in determining the appropriate compensation levels for our executive officers. Overall, Compensia's analysis of our Peer Group indicated that the target total cash compensation for our then-serving named executive officers was at or below the 30th percentile of the companies in our Peer Group. When equity compensation was factored in, based on the "initial equity value" described below and without taking into account the effect of the deferred vesting start dates that are applicable to certain of the equity compensation awards of our named executive officers, the target total direct compensation for our then-serving named executive officers, other than our CEO, was between the 70th percentile relative to the companies in our Peer Group and the top of our Peer Group.

In the second quarter of 2019, the compensation, nominating & governance committee reviewed the selection criteria and the companies in our Peer Group. Following that review, the compensation, nominating & governance committee decided to remove Twenty-First Century Fox and add Uber Technologies. The compensation, nominating & governance committee believes our updated Peer Group reflects the current competitive and talent environment. Accordingly, we plan to use the following list of companies in our Peer Group for the 2020 executive compensation process:

Alphabet	Microsoft
Amazon.com	Netflix
Apple	PayPal Holdings
AT&T	salesforce.com
CBS	The Walt Disney Company
Cisco Systems	Uber Technologies
Comcast	Verizon Communications

The compensation, nominating & governance committee expects to periodically review and update our Peer Group and the underlying criteria as our business and market environment continue to evolve.

[...]

Perquisites and Other Benefits

Consistent with the practices of many companies in our Peer Group, we provide certain perquisites to our named executive officers for the reasons described below. In approving these perquisites, our compensation, nominating & governance committee considered comparative Peer Group and other market data provided by Compensia.

Because of the high visibility of our company, our compensation, nominating & governance committee has authorized an "overall security program" for Mr. Zuckerberg to address safety concerns due to specific threats to his safety arising directly as a result of his position as our founder, CEO, Chairman, and controlling stockholder. Our compensation, nominating & governance committee has also authorized a security program for Ms. Sandberg, including certain personal security measures, to address safety concerns resulting from her position as our COO. We require these security measures for the company's benefit because of the importance of Mr. Zuckerberg and Ms. Sandberg to Facebook, and we believe that the scope and costs of these security programs are appropriate and necessary.

Our compensation, nominating & governance committee evaluates these security programs at least annually, including a review of security professional assessments of safety threats and recommendations for the security programs. Since the implementation of Mr. Zuckerberg's overall security program, each of these assessments has identified specific threats to Mr. Zuckerberg as a result of the high-profile nature of being our founder, CEO, Chairman, and controlling stockholder. We believe that Mr. Zuckerberg's role puts him in a unique position: he is synonymous with Facebook and, as a result, negative sentiment regarding our company is directly associated with, and often transferred to, Mr. Zuckerberg. Mr. Zuckerberg is one of the most-recognized executives in the world, in large part as a result of the size of our user base and our continued exposure to global media, legislative, and regulatory attention.

Under Mr. Zuckerberg's overall security program, we pay for costs related to personal security for Mr. Zuckerberg at his residences and during personal travel, including the annual costs of security personnel for his protection and the procurement, installation, and maintenance of certain security measures for his residences. We also provide an annual pre-tax allowance of $10 million to Mr. Zuckerberg to cover additional costs related to his and his family's personal security. This allowance is paid to Mr. Zuckerberg net of required tax withholdings, and Mr. Zuckerberg must apply the net amount towards additional personnel, equipment, services, residential improvements, or other security-related costs. Although Mr. Zuckerberg expects to use the full net amount during each calendar year in which the allowance is paid, he may apply any unused portion of the allowance for a given year to cover excess security-related costs in future years or prior years (no earlier than 2018).

In addition, Mr. Zuckerberg uses private aircraft for personal travel in connection with his overall security program. On certain occasions, Mr. Zuckerberg may be accompanied by guests when using private aircraft. Although we do not consider Mr. Zuckerberg's overall security program to be a perquisite for his benefit for the reasons described above, the costs related to personal security for Mr. Zuckerberg at his residences and during personal travel pursuant to his overall security program, as well as the annual security allowance and the costs of private aircraft for personal travel, are reported as other compensation to Mr. Zuckerberg in the "All Other Compensation" column of the "—2019 Summary Compensation Table" below. The costs of Mr. Zuckerberg's security program vary from year to year depending on requisite security measures, his travel schedule, and other factors. Increased costs in 2019 were primarily due to regular personal travel and market increases in the costs of security personnel. The compensation, nominating & governance committee believes that these costs are appropriate and necessary in light of the threat landscape and the fact that Mr. Zuckerberg has requested to receive only $1 in annual salary and does not receive any bonus payments, equity awards, or other incentive compensation.

Our security professional assessments have also identified specific threats to Ms. Sandberg as a result of her high-profile role as our COO. Under Ms. Sandberg's security program, we pay for costs related to personal security for Ms. Sandberg at her residence and during personal travel, including the annual costs of security personnel for her protection. In addition, Ms. Sandberg uses private aircraft for personal travel in connection with her security program and may be accompanied by guests when using private aircraft on certain occasions. The costs related to personal security for Ms. Sandberg, as well as the costs of private aircraft for personal travel, are reported as other compensation to Ms. Sandberg in the "All Other Compensation" column of the "—2019 Summary Compensation Table" below. The costs of Ms. Sandberg's security program vary from year to year depending on requisite security measures, her travel schedule, and other factors. Increased costs in 2019 were primarily due to regular personal travel, additional residential security coverage, and market increases in the costs of security personnel.

From time to time, we also provide certain personal security measures to other executive officers in response to specific security threats in light of their roles at our company, including pre-tax security allowances and certain costs related to personal security at their residences. The costs related to personal security for our executive officers are reported as other compensation to them in the "All Other Compensation" column of the "—2019 Summary Compensation Table" below.

In 2019, we also paid for relocation services, including a gross-up for taxable relocation services, to Ms. Newstead to assist with relocating near company headquarters in connection with her hiring. The costs related to these relocation services are reported as other compensation to Ms. Newstead in the "All Other Compensation" column of the "—2019 Summary Compensation Table" below.

2019 Say on Pay Vote

We held a non-binding advisory stockholder vote on the compensation program for our named executive officers, commonly referred to as a "say on pay" vote, at our 2019 Annual Meeting of Stockholders. Over 90% of the voting power of shares voted at the 2019 Annual Meeting of Stockholders were cast in favor of our say on pay proposal. Our compensation, nominating & governance committee considered the result of this advisory vote to be an endorsement of our compensation program, policies, practices, and philosophy for our named executive officers. Our compensation, nominating & governance committee will continue to consider the outcome of our say on pay votes and our stockholder views when making compensation decisions for our named executive officers.

Based on the results of a separate non-binding advisory stockholder vote on the frequency of future stockholder advisory votes regarding the compensation program for our named executive officers, commonly referred to as a "say on frequency" vote, held at our 2019 Annual Meeting of Stockholders, our board of directors determined that we will hold our say on pay vote every three years until the next required say on frequency vote. Our next say on pay vote will occur no later than 2022 and our next say on frequency vote will occur no later than 2025.

[...]

Limitations on Liability and Indemnification Matters

Our restated certificate of incorporation contains provisions that limit the liability of our directors for monetary damages to the fullest extent permitted by the Delaware General Corporation Law. Consequently, our directors will not be personally liable to us or our stockholders for monetary damages for any breach of fiduciary duties as directors, except liability for:

- any breach of the director's duty of loyalty to us or our stockholders;
- any act or omission not in good faith or that involves intentional misconduct or a knowing violation of law;
- unlawful payments of dividends or unlawful stock repurchases or redemptions as provided in Section 174 of the Delaware General Corporation Law; or
- any transaction from which the director derived an improper personal benefit.

Our restated certificate of incorporation and amended and restated bylaws require us to indemnify our directors and executive officers made or threatened to be made a party to an action or proceeding, by reason of the fact that he or she serves or served in such capacity at our request to the maximum extent not prohibited by the Delaware General Corporation Law or any other applicable law and allow us to indemnify other officers, employees, and other agents as set forth in the Delaware General Corporation Law or any other applicable law.

We have entered, and intend to continue to enter, into separate indemnification agreements with our directors, executive officers, and other key employees, in addition to the indemnification provided for in our restated certificate of incorporation, amended and restated bylaws and other applicable law. These agreements, among other things, require us to indemnify our directors, executive officers, and other key employees for certain expenses, including attorneys' fees, judgments, penalties, fines, and settlement amounts actually and reasonably incurred by such person in any action or proceeding arising out of their services to us, or any of our subsidiaries or any other company or enterprise to which the person provides services at our request, including liability arising out of negligence or active or passive wrongdoing by the officer, director or employee. We believe that these charter provisions and indemnification agreements are necessary to attract and retain qualified persons such as directors, officers and key employees. We also maintain directors' and officers' liability insurance.

The limitation of liability and indemnification provisions in our restated certificate of incorporation and amended and restated bylaws may discourage stockholders from bringing a lawsuit against our directors and officers for breach of their fiduciary duty. They may also reduce the likelihood of derivative litigation against our directors and officers, even though an action, if successful, might benefit us and other stockholders. Further, a stockholder's investment may be adversely affected to the extent that we pay the costs of settlement and damage awards against directors and officers as required by these indemnification provisions.

Insofar as indemnification for liabilities arising under the Securities Act of 1933, as amended (Securities Act), may be permitted to directors, executive officers or persons controlling us, we have been informed that in the opinion of the SEC such indemnification is against public policy as expressed in the Securities Act and is therefore unenforceable.

[...]

STOCKHOLDER ENGAGEMENT AND COMMUNICATIONS

At Facebook, we believe that effective corporate governance includes regular, transparent, and constructive communication with our stockholders to understand their perspectives and answer their inquiries. Throughout the year, we engage with a significant portion of our stockholders, including our top institutional investors. Through these outreach efforts, we discuss a variety of topics of interest to our stockholders, including, among other things, our operating and financial performance, strategy, products, corporate governance, and important environmental and social issues. We do this as part of our commitment to maintain an active dialogue with stockholders, be responsive, and hear their viewpoints, constructive insights into emerging issues, and feedback on our efforts. More information about investor relations is available on our website at *https://investor.fb.com*.

Stockholders may contact our board of directors about bona fide issues or questions about Facebook by sending a letter to the following address: c/o Facebook, Inc., 1601 Willow Road, Menlo Park, California, 94025, Attention: Board of Directors. Each communication should specify the applicable addressee or addressees to be contacted, the general topic of the communication, and the class and number of shares of our stock that are owned of record (if a record holder) or beneficially. If a stockholder wishes to contact the independent members of the board of directors, the stockholder should address such communication to the attention of the Lead Independent Director at the address above. Our legal department will initially receive and process communications before forwarding them to the addressee, and generally will not forward a communication that is unrelated to the duties and responsibilities of the board of directors, including communications the legal department determines to be primarily commercial in nature, related to an improper or irrelevant topic, or a request for general information about the company, its products, or services. In addition, material that is unduly hostile, threatening, illegal, or similarly unsuitable will be excluded, with the provision that any communication that is filtered out must be made available to any non-management director upon request.

GOVERNANCE, TRANSPARENCY, AND DIVERSITY AT FACEBOOK

Governance

We are committed to sound corporate governance practices and encouraging effective policy and decision making at both the board of directors and management level.

We publish our governance documents on our website at *http://investor.fb.com/governance.cfm*, including our certificate of incorporation, bylaws, committee charters, corporate governance guidelines, code of conduct, stock ownership guidelines, and approach to tax policy. Our corporate governance guidelines serve as a framework to assist our board of directors in the exercise of its governance responsibilities, and address board and committee composition, responsibilities, and compensation, among other matters. Our code of conduct provides guidelines for business conduct and applies to members of our board of directors, our executive officers, employees, contractors, consultants, and others working on our behalf. We intend to satisfy the disclosure requirement under Item 5.05 of Form 8-K regarding amendment to, or waiver from, a provision of our code of conduct by posting such information on our website at the address specified above.

Transparency

Transparency allows people to hold us accountable and judge our progress. We are committed to increasing transparency across our business.

Our goal is to make Facebook a place for open and authentic communication, while safeguarding people's private information and keeping our platform safe for everyone. We publish our Community Standards to help people understand our policies and what type of content is allowed on Facebook. Since 2018, we have also published internal guidelines our teams use to enforce those standards. In 2019, we also introduced a section on our Community Standards website where people can track recent policy updates we have made. Our comprehensive Community Standards are available at *https://facebook.com/communitystandards*.

We publish regular reports to give our community visibility into how we enforce policies, respond to data requests, protect intellectual property, and monitor temporary Internet disruptions that impact the availability of Facebook products. Our Transparency Reports are available at *https://transparency.facebook.com*. Our Community Standards Enforcement Reports track our progress on enforcing our content policies and are available at *https://transparency.facebook.com/community-standards*-enforcement. In this twice-annual report, we disclose the prevalence of violating content, the amount of content we take action on, and the amount of content we find proactively before people report it. We also hold conference calls with media after we issue each such report.

We also regularly post company updates in our Newsroom at *https://newsroom.fb.com* and on Mark Zuckerberg's Facebook Page at *https://www.facebook.com/zuck*.

Diversity & Inclusion

Diversity and inclusion are core to everything we do at Facebook. We work to build a diverse and inclusive workplace where we can leverage our collective cognitive diversity to build the best products and make the best decisions for the global community we serve. We have made progress, but we still have more work to do.

We have made steady progress in increasing representation of women globally in technical, non-technical, and leadership roles, and have made some progress on increasing the numbers of Black and Hispanic people in non-technical roles in the U.S. For example, since 2014, we have increased the number of Black women at Facebook by a factor of 25 and the number of Black men by a factor of 10. We continue to focus on increasing the number of underrepresented people in technical and leadership roles. We publish our global gender diversity and U.S. ethnic diversity workforce data annually. Our Diversity Report for 2019 provides additional background about our journey and the progress we are making, and is available at *https://about.fb.com/news/2019/07/2019-diversity-report/*.

To support our goals of diversifying our workforce, we globally rolled out our Diverse Slate Approach, which ensures that teams and hiring managers have the opportunity to consider qualified underrepresented people for open roles. We have seen steady increases in hiring rates for underrepresented people since we started testing this approach in 2015. We also continue to expand our recruiting team and develop internship programs for women and underrepresented people. Over 700 students have graduated from Facebook University (FBU), our training program for college freshmen and sophomores from underrepresented groups with an interest in Computer Science. Over 1,000 students have participated in the program in five different hiring pipelines (Software Engineering, Analytics, Product

Design, Operations and Sales/Advertising) and many have returned to work at Facebook.

We have an obligation to build a culture of inclusion where everyone can thrive. This means each individual can have an impact and be productive in part because they are working in an environment where they are seen, heard, and valued. Inclusion is a choice, and we want everyone at Facebook to behave inclusively.

Our strategies are focused on ensuring that underrepresented people receive consistent support in terms of their onboarding, performance, and career development, and feel a sense of belonging in our community. We are also focused on increasing the diversity and inclusion capabilities of managers and leaders to build inclusive teams, departments, and organizations so that our products and community will benefit from the diverse perspectives of our people.

We believe retention, people development, and inclusion are just as crucial as recruiting. This is why we invest in our thriving Facebook Resource Groups and our annual Community events such as Women's Community Summit, Black Community Summit, Latin Community Summit, and Pride Community Summit. These all help build community and support professional development. They are designed to empower, inspire, and provide resources to help our people grow professionally. We encourage all employees to take our "Managing Unconscious Bias" training to help reduce the effects of bias in the workplace and to help employees better understand diverse perspectives. Since 2015, we have made this training available publicly at *https://managingbias.fb.com* and have added two programs, Managing Inclusion and Be The Ally. Managing Inclusion trains managers to understand the issues that affect underrepresented communities and to actively solicit input from people who may feel excluded. Be The Ally gives everyone at Facebook the common language, tools, and space to identify when someone may be experiencing bias and to stand up in support of them.

We are committed to a policy of inclusiveness and to pursuing diversity in terms of background and perspective when evaluating candidates for membership on our board of directors. Under our corporate governance guidelines, it is the policy of our compensation, nominating & governance committee to consider candidates with diverse backgrounds in terms of knowledge, experience, skills, and other characteristics, and to ensure that the initial list of candidates from which new director nominees are chosen includes candidates with a diversity of race, ethnicity, and gender. Our corporate governance guidelines are available at *http://investor.fb.com/governance.cfm*.

We are also committed to promoting diversity among the companies that do business with Facebook. We believe that having diverse suppliers helps us build better products for our global community. Through our Supplier Diversity Program, we connect qualified diverse-owned businesses to our community while also helping these companies grow their businesses by using our platform, products, and services. We publish information on our Supplier Diversity Program at *https://www.facebook.com/suppliers/diversity.*

[...]

PROPOSAL ONE: ELECTION OF DIRECTORS

The following individuals are nominated for election to the board of directors at the Annual Meeting, all of whom are currently serving on our board of directors:

- Peggy Alford
- Marc L. Andreessen
- Andrew W. Houston
- Nancy Killefer
- Robert M. Kimmitt
- Sheryl K. Sandberg
- Peter A. Thiel
- Tracey T. Travis
- Mark Zuckerberg

Directors will be elected by a plurality of the votes of the shares of our Class A common stock and Class B common stock present or represented by proxy at the 2020 Annual Meeting of Stockholders and entitled to vote on the election of directors, which means that the nine nominees receiving the highest number of affirmative votes will be elected. If elected, each of these individuals will serve until the next annual meeting of stockholders and until his or her successor has been elected and qualified, or until his or her earlier death, resignation, or removal. In the event that any nominee for any reason is unable or unwilling to stand for election, the proxies will be voted for such substitute nominee as our board of directors may determine or we may adjust the authorized number of directors of the board. Messrs. Chenault and Zients, who are currently serving on our board of directors, are not standing for re-election at the Annual Meeting and their terms as directors will end at the Annual Meeting. We thank Messrs. Chenault and Zients for their distinguished service.

Our compensation, nominating & governance committee retained a search firm to assist in the process of identifying and evaluating potential director candidates and conducted the searches for new directors in accordance with the board diversity policy set forth in our corporate governance guidelines. Additionally, our compensation, nominating & governance committee solicited input from management, our board of directors, and others. As to the new members of our board of directors, Mr. Houston was recommended by our CEO, Ms. Killefer was recommended by a member of management, and each of Ambassador Kimmitt and Ms. Travis was recommended by a non-management director.

Unless otherwise provided by law, any vacancy on the board of directors, including a vacancy created by an increase in the authorized number of directors, may be filled by the stockholders, by a majority of the directors then in office, even if less than a quorum, or by a sole remaining director.

The relevant experiences, qualifications, attributes, or skills of each nominee that led our board of directors to recommend the above persons as a nominee for director are described in the section of this proxy statement entitled "Executive Officers, Directors, and Corporate Governance."

The board of directors recommends a vote FOR the election of each of the nominated directors.

[...]

STOCKHOLDER PROPOSALS

Proposals Four through Eleven (the Stockholder Proposals) are proposals we received from our stockholders. If the proponents of these proposals, or representatives who are qualified under state law, are present at our Annual Meeting and submit the proposals for a vote, then the proposals will be voted upon. The Stockholder Proposals, including any supporting statements, are included exactly as submitted to us by the proponents of these proposals. The board of directors' recommendation on each proposal is presented immediately following our opposing statement to the proposal.

SEC rules require that we provide the proponents with a copy of our opposing statement to their proposal at least 30 days prior to filing definitive copies of our proxy statement and form of proxy with the SEC. Accordingly, we provided the proponents with copies of our opposing statements by March 11, 2020.

We will promptly provide you with the name, address, and, to our knowledge, the number of voting securities held by the proponents of the Stockholder Proposals, upon receiving a written or oral request directed to:

Facebook, Inc., 1601 Willow Road, Menlo Park, California 94025, Attention: Corporate Secretary.

PROPOSAL FOUR: STOCKHOLDER PROPOSAL REGARDING CHANGE IN STOCKHOLDER VOTING

Give Each Share an Equal Vote

RESOLVED: Shareholders request that our Board take all practicable steps in its control to initiate and adopt a recapitalization plan for all outstanding stock to have one vote per share. We recommend that this be done through a phase-out process in which the board would, within seven years or other timeframe justified by the board, establish fair and appropriate mechanisms through which disproportionate rights of Class B shareholders could be eliminated. This is not intended to unnecessarily limit our Board's judgment in crafting the requested change in accordance with applicable laws and existing contracts.

SUPPORTING STATEMENT: In 2019, Facebook was fined $5 billion by the Federal Trade Commission for mishandling users' personal information. This followed a tumultuous year of scandals that has resulted in the loss of users, decline in user confidence, and included a one-day stock price drop that wiped off "more than $119bn ... [from] Facebook's market value" in July 2018. The public scandals that have caused this loss in shareholder value came from management and Board decisions that have not protected shareholder investment.

In allowing certain stock more voting power, our company takes public shareholder money but does not provide all shareholders an equal voice in our company's governance, and therefore severely limits shareholders' ability to provide effective feedback to management and the board. Founder Mark Zuckerberg controls over 53% of the vote, though he owns less than 13% of the economic value of the firm.

Without equal voting rights, shareholders cannot hold management accountable. This is exemplified by the 2016 attempt by Facebook to create a non-voting class of stock. Described as a move to ensure that Mr. Zuckerberg retained control of our Company, the new class of stock was approved at the annual meeting despite the fact that almost 1.5 *billion* shares of stock voted AGAINST its creation. Only threat of a lawsuit «by shareholders who claimed that conflicts of interest and other behind-the-scenes discussions tainted a board decision to approve the creation of a new class of shares» was able to incite reversal of the plan.

Facebook's 10-K describes the risk of the current share system: "Mr. Zuckerberg is entitled to vote his shares...in his own interests, which may not always be in the interests of our stockholders generally."

The Council for Institutional Investors (CII) recommends a seven year phase-out of dual class share offerings. The International Corporate Governance Network supports CII's recommendation "to require to a time-based sunset clause for dual class shares to revert to a traditional one-share/one-vote structure no more than seven years after a company's IPO date."

Fake news, election interference, and threats to our democracy—shareholders need more than deny, deflect, and delay from our Company's management. We urge shareholders to vote FOR a recapitalization plan for all outstanding stock to have one vote per share.

FACEBOOK OPPOSING STATEMENT

We are focused on our mission to give people the power to build community and bring the world closer together. If we focus on this mission and build useful and engaging products and services, we believe we will create the most value for our stockholders over the long term. Our board of directors believes that our capital structure contributes to our stability and insulates our board of directors and management from short-term pressures, which allows them to focus on our mission and long-term success.

The vision and leadership of our founder and CEO, Mark Zuckerberg, has guided us from our inception. Mr. Zuckerberg is invested in our long-term success, and under his guidance we have established a track record of creating value for our stockholders and navigating important opportunities and challenges. For example, our concerted efforts to improve the privacy, safety, and security of our community have required significant investment, which has impacted our profitability. This level of investment may not have been possible if our board of directors and CEO were focused on short-term success over the long-term interests of our community and our company.

A substantial majority of the members of our board of directors are independent under applicable SEC and Nasdaq rules, we have recently added several new independent directors, and each of the committees of our board of directors is comprised entirely of independent directors. We believe the independent members of our board of directors provide effective oversight and represent the interests of all stockholders.

The dual class capital structure with two classes of common stock (Class A common stock with one vote per share and Class B common stock with ten votes per share) was implemented in 2009, well before our initial public offering, and all of our investors who purchased shares of our Class A common stock in, and after, our initial public offering were aware of our capital structure, which is disclosed in detail in our public filings with the SEC.

In addition, our stockholders rejected a substantially similar proposal at each of our last six annual meetings of our stockholders.

We believe that our capital structure is in the best interests of our stockholders and that our current corporate governance structure is sound and effective. Therefore, our board of directors recommends that our stockholders vote against this proposal.

The board of directors recommends a vote AGAINST the stockholder proposal.

PROPOSAL FIVE: STOCKHOLDER PROPOSAL REGARDING AN INDEPENDENT CHAIR

Independent Board Chairperson

Resolved: Shareholders request the Board of Directors adopt as policy, and amend the bylaws as necessary, to require henceforth that the Chair of the Board of Directors, whenever possible, be an independent member of the Board. This independence policy shall apply prospectively so as not to violate any contractual obligations. If the Board determines that a Chair who was independent when selected is no longer independent, the Board shall select a new Chair who satisfies the requirements of the policy within a reasonable amount of time. Compliance with this policy is waived if no independent director is available and willing to serve as Chair.

Supporting Statement: Facebook CEO Mark Zuckerberg has been Board Chair since 2012. His dual-class shareholdings give him approximately 58% of Facebook's voting shares while holding only 13% of the economic interest, leaving the board, even with a lead independent director, with only a limited ability to check Mr. Zuckerberg's power. We believe this weakens Facebook's governance and oversight of management. Selecting an independent Chair would free the CEO to focus on managing the Company and enable the Chairperson to focus on oversight and strategic guidance.

Facebook has resisted recent shareholder requests to separate these roles. At the 2019 annual meeting, according to our calculations, this proposal received the support of 68% of the votes cast when excluding the shares of 13 executives and board members. However, the board has not acted on this important signal from its non-insider shareholders.

Alphabet, Microsoft, Apple, and Autodesk all have separate CEO and chairperson roles.

We believe this lack of independent board Chair and oversight has contributed to Facebook missing, or mishandling, a number of severe controversies, increasing risk exposure and costs to shareholders.

Concentrating power in the hands of one person—any person—is unwise. Looking forward to future growth opportunities, we believe Facebook needs strong risk oversight and to rebuild trust with investors, employees, users, and regulators. Transitioning to an independent board chair is necessary to rebuild the company's reputation and to create a governance environment with the benefits of genuine accountability and meaningful oversight.

FACEBOOK OPPOSING STATEMENT

We believe that our current board structure is effective in supporting strong board leadership. Implementing the proposal is unnecessary because the leadership structure of our board of directors already provides for independent leadership and oversight of management. Susan D. Desmond-Hellmann served as our Lead Independent Director from 2015 to 2019, and our independent directors recently designated Ambassador Kimmitt to serve as Lead Independent Director upon his appointment to our board of directors in March 2020. Our Lead Independent Director role includes the following authority and responsibilities, as described in greater detail in the section of this proxy statement entitled "Executive Officers, Directors, and Corporate Governance":

- presiding at all meetings of the board of directors at which the Chairman is not present, including executive sessions of the independent directors;
- calling separate meetings of the independent directors or special meetings of the full board of directors;
- facilitating discussion and open dialogue among the independent directors during meetings of the board of directors, executive sessions, and otherwise;
- serving as principal liaison between the independent directors and the Chairman;
- providing the Chairman with feedback and counsel concerning his interactions with the board of directors;

- providing leadership to the board of directors if circumstances arise in which the role of the Chairman may be, or may be perceived to be, in conflict;
- coordinating with the Chairman to set the agenda for meetings of the board of directors, taking into account input from other independent directors; and
- leading our board of directors in governance matters in coordination with our compensation, nominating & governance committee, including the evaluation of the performance of the CEO, the selection of committee chairs and memberships, and our annual board of directors and committee self-evaluations.

We believe that the role of the Lead Independent Director facilitates effective representation of the interests of all stockholders. Further, we have recently appointed several new independent directors, a substantial majority of our directors are independent, and each of the committees of our board of directors is comprised entirely of independent directors.

Our board of directors currently has no established policy on whether or not to have a non-executive Chair and believes that it should make that judgment based on circumstances and experience. Our board of directors currently believes that the most effective leadership model is that Mr. Zuckerberg, our founder and controlling stockholder, serves as both Chairman and CEO. We believe our board of directors is functioning effectively under its current structure, and that the current structure provides appropriate oversight protections. We do not believe that requiring the Chair to be independent will provide appreciably better direction and performance, and instead could cause inefficiency in board and management function and relations.

In addition, our stockholders rejected a similar proposal at our annual meetings of stockholders in 2017 and 2019.

We believe that our current board structure is in the best interests of our stockholders. Therefore, our board of directors recommends that our stockholders vote against this proposal.

The board of directors recommends a vote AGAINST the stockholder proposal.

PROPOSAL SIX: STOCKHOLDER PROPOSAL REGARDING MAJORITY VOTING FOR DIRECTORS

Proposal 6—Directors to be Elected by Majority Vote

Resolved: Shareholders hereby request that our Board of Directors initiate the appropriate process as soon as possible to amend our Company's articles of incorporation and/or bylaws to provide that director nominees shall be elected by the affirmative vote of the majority of votes cast at an annual meeting of shareholders, with a plurality vote standard retained for contested director elections, that is, when the number of director nominees exceeds the number of board seats. This proposal includes that a director who receives less than such a majority vote be removed from the board immediately or as soon as a replacement director can be qualified on an expedited basis. If such a director has key experience, they can transition to being a consultant or a director emeritus.

Supporting Statement: To provide shareholders a meaningful role in director elections, our Company's current director election standard should be changed from a plurality vote standard to a majority vote standard where only board nominated candidates are on the ballot.

This will establish a more meaningful vote standard for board nominees and could lead to improved performance. Under our Company's current voting system, a director can be elected if all shareholders oppose the director but one shareholder votes FOR, if even by mistake.

More than 89% of the companies in the S&P 500 have adopted majority voting for uncontested elections, as have 67% of the S&P 1500.

BlackRock's proxy voting guidelines include the following: "Majority voting standards assist in ensuring that directors who are not broadly supported by shareholders are not elected to serve as their representatives." Among our Company's largest shareholders: T. Rowe Price Associates and BlackRock both voted FOR 88.9% of shareholder proposals on this topic. SSgA Funds Management voted FOR 100% of such proposals.

Facebook operates essentially as a dictatorship. Mark Zuckerberg controls a majority of the votes using a multi-class share structure with unequal voting rights. Shareholders cannot elect directors annually, call special meetings and have no right to act by written consent. A supermajority vote is required to amend certain bylaws. Our Board is locked into an out-dated governance structure that reduces board accountability to shareholders. Reform is needed.

Facebook's autocratic corporate governance is spilling into civil society. Facebook may profit in the short-term from ads full of lies about Brexit and

(Continued)

presidential candidates. See https://youtu.be/OQSMr-3GGvQ and https://youtu.be/gfN2_LRv54w?t=9 However, such irresponsible policies are likely to lead a backlash, such as a breakup or heavy regulations.

Fake news, election interference, threats to our bottom line and our democracy. Shareholders need more than deny; deflect, and delay. We need a real voice through governance reforms, including Majority Vote requirements to elect directors. Please vote FOR.

Directors to be Elected by Majority Vote—Proposal 6

FACEBOOK OPPOSING STATEMENT

Given our status as a controlled company, there is not a significant practical difference between majority voting and plurality voting for the election of directors. Accordingly, we believe that deviating from the plurality voting standard is unnecessary at this time. However, our compensation, nominating & governance committee will continue to evaluate the appropriate voting standard for the election of directors.

The policy of our board of directors is to encourage the selection of directors who will contribute to our success and our mission to give people the power to build community and bring the world closer together. As described in greater detail in the section of this proxy statement entitled "Executive Officers, Directors, and Corporate Governance," our compensation, nominating & governance committee is responsible for nominating members for election to our board of directors and has established policies and procedures to consider candidates with diverse backgrounds in terms of knowledge, experience, skills, and other characteristics, including candidates recommended by directors, stockholders, management, and others.

In addition, our stockholders rejected a similar proposal at our annual meeting of stockholders in 2019.

We believe that our capital structure is in the best interests of our stockholders and that our current corporate governance structure is sound and effective. Therefore, our board of directors recommends that our stockholders vote against this proposal.

The board of directors recommends a vote AGAINST the stockholder proposal.

[...]

[illegible]

SCAN TO
VIEW MATERIALS & VOTE

VOTE BY INTERNET
Before The Meeting - **www.proxyvote.com or scan the QR Barcode above**

[illegible]

During The Meeting - **www.virtualshareholdermeeting.com/FB2020**

[illegible] XXXX XXXX XXXX XXXX [illegible]

VOTE BY PHONE - 1-800-690-6903

[illegible]

VOTE BY MAIL

[illegible]

TO VOTE, MARK BLOCKS BELOW IN BLUE OR BLACK INK AS FOLLOWS:

D08583-P33136 KEEP THIS PORTION FOR YOUR RECORDS

DETACH AND RETURN THIS PORTION ONLY

THIS PROXY CARD IS VALID ONLY WHEN SIGNED AND DATED.

FACEBOOK, INC.

The Board of Directors recommends you vote FOR the following:

	For All	Withhold All	For All Except
1. Election of Directors	☐	☐	☐

Nominees:

01) Peggy Alford
02) Marc L. Andreessen
03) Andrew W. Houston
04) Nancy Killefer
05) Robert M. Kimmitt
06) Sheryl K. Sandberg
07) Peter A. Thiel
08) Tracey T. Travis
09) Mark Zuckerberg

To withhold authority to vote for any individual nominee(s), mark "For All Except" and write the number(s) of the nominee(s) on the line below.

____

The Board of Directors recommends you vote FOR the following proposals:

	For	Against	Abstain
2. To ratify the appointment of Ernst & Young LLP as Facebook, Inc.'s independent registered public accounting firm for the fiscal year ending December 31, 2020.	☐	☐	☐
3. To approve the director compensation policy.	☐	☐	☐

The Board of Directors recommends you vote AGAINST the following proposals:

	For	Against	Abstain
4. A stockholder proposal regarding change in stockholder voting.	☐	☐	☐
5. A stockholder proposal regarding an independent chair.	☐	☐	☐
6. A stockholder proposal regarding majority voting for directors.	☐	☐	☐
7. A stockholder proposal regarding political advertising.	☐	☐	☐
8. A stockholder proposal regarding human/civil rights expert on board.	☐	☐	☐
9. A stockholder proposal regarding report on civil and human rights risks.	☐	☐	☐
10. A stockholder proposal regarding child exploitation.	☐	☐	☐
11. A stockholder proposal regarding median gender/racial pay gap.	☐	☐	☐

Please sign exactly as your name(s) appear(s) hereon. When signing as attorney, executor, administrator, or other fiduciary, please give full title as such. Joint owners should each sign personally. All holders must sign. If a corporation or partnership, please sign in full corporate or partnership name by authorized officer.

Signature [PLEASE SIGN WITHIN BOX] Date

Signature (Joint Owners) Date

Important Notice Regarding the Availability of Proxy Materials for the Annual Meeting:
The Notice and Proxy Statement and Annual Report are available at www.proxyvote.com.

D08584-P33136

FACEBOOK, INC.
Annual Meeting of Stockholders
May 27, 2020 10:00 a.m. Pacific Time

This proxy is solicited by the Board of Directors

The undersigned hereby appoints David M. Wehner and Jennifer G. Newstead, and each of them, as proxy holders with full power of substitution and authority to act in the absence of the other, each to vote with respect to shares of the Company's capital stock for which proxies will be solicited for use in connection with the Annual Meeting of Stockholders, to be held live via the Internet at www.virtualshareholdermeeting.com/FB2020 at 10:00 a.m. Pacific Time on May 27, 2020, and at any adjournments or postponements thereof.

This proxy, when properly executed, will be voted in the manner directed herein. If no such direction is made, this proxy will be voted in accordance with the Board of Directors' recommendations.

Continued and to be signed on reverse side

DOCUMENT FIVE

Certificate of Merger

CA FORM: OBE MERG

http://bpd.cdn.sos.ca.gov/corp/pdf/mergers/corp-merger.pdf

"OBE MERG: Certificate of Approval / Certificate of Merger," http://bpd.cdn.sos.ca.gov/corp/pdf/mergers/corp-merger.pdf, State of California, 2016.

(Continued)

OBE MERG

State of California
Secretary of State
Certificate of Merger

(California Corporations Code sections 1113(g), 3203(g), 6019.1, 8019.1, 9640, 12540.1, 15911.14, 16915(b) and 17710.14)

IMPORTANT—Read all instructions before completing this form.

This Space For Filing Use Only

1. NAME OF SURVIVING ENTITY	2. TYPE OF ENTITY	3. CA SECRETARY OF STATE FILE NUMBER	4. JURISDICTION
5. NAME OF DISAPPEARING ENTITY	6. TYPE OF ENTITY	7. CA SECRETARY OF STATE FILE NUMBER	8. JURISDICTION

9. THE PRINCIPAL TERMS OF THE AGREEMENT OF MERGER WERE APPROVED BY A VOTE OF THE NUMBER OF INTERESTS OR SHARES OF EACH CLASS THAT EQUALED OR EXCEEDED THE VOTE REQUIRED. *(IF A VOTE WAS REQUIRED, SPECIFY THE CLASS AND THE NUMBER OF OUTSTANDING INTERESTS OF EACH CLASS ENTITLED TO VOTE ON THE MERGER AND THE PERCENTAGE VOTE REQUIRED OF EACH CLASS. ATTACH ADDITIONAL PAGES, IF NEEDED.)*

SURVIVING ENTITY	DISAPPEARING ENTITY
CLASS AND NUMBER **AND** PERCENTAGE VOTE REQUIRED	CLASS AND NUMBER **AND** PERCENTAGE VOTE REQUIRED

10. IF EQUITY SECURITIES OF A PARENT PARTY ARE TO BE ISSUED IN THE MERGER, CHECK THE APPLICABLE STATEMENT.

- ☐ No vote of the shareholders of the parent party was required.
- ☐ The required vote of the shareholders of the parent party was obtained.

11. IF THE SURVIVING ENTITY IS A DOMESTIC LIMITED LIABLITY COMPANY, LIMITED PARTNERSHIP, OR PARTNERSHIP, PROVIDE THE REQUISITE CHANGES (IF ANY) TO THE INFORMATION SET FORTH IN THE SURVIVING ENTITY'S ARTICLES OF ORGANIZATION, CERTIFICATE OF LIMITED PARTNERSHIP OR STATEMENT OF PARTNERSHIP AUTHORITY RESULTING FROM THE MERGER. ATTACH ADDITIONAL PAGES, IF NECESSARY.

12 IF A DISAPPEARING ENTITY IS A DOMESTIC LIMITED LIABLITY COMPANY, LIMITED PARTNERSHIP, OR PARTNERSHIP, AND THE SURVIVING ENTITY IS NOT A DOMESTIC ENTITY OF THE SAME TYPE, ENTER THE PRINCIPAL ADDRESS OF THE SURVIVING ENTITY.

PRINCIPAL ADDRESS OF SURVIVING ENTITY	CITY AND STATE	ZIP CODE

13. OTHER INFORMATION REQUIRED TO BE STATED IN THE CERTIFICATE OF MERGER BY THE LAWS UNDER WHICH EACH CONSTITUENT OTHER BUSINESS ENTITY IS ORGANIZED. ATTACH ADDITIONAL PAGES, IF NECESSARY.

14. STATUTORY OR OTHER BASIS UNDER WHICH A FOREIGN OTHER BUSINESS ENTITY IS AUTHORIZED TO EFFECT THE MERGER.

15. FUTURE EFFECTIVE DATE, IF ANY

_________ - _________ - _________
(Month) (Day) (Year)

16. ADDITIONAL INFORMATION SET FORTH ON ATTACHED PAGES, IF ANY, IS INCORPORATED HEREIN BY THIS REFERENCE AND MADE PART OF THIS CERTIFICATE.

17. I CERTIFY UNDER PENALTY OF PERJURY UNDER THE LAWS OF THE STATE OF CALIFORNIA THAT THE FOREGOING IS TRUE AND CORRECT OF MY OWN KNOWLEDGE. I DECLARE I AM THE PERSON WHO EXECUTED THIS INSTRUMENT, WHICH EXECUTION IS MY ACT AND DEED.

SIGNATURE OF AUTHORIZED PERSON FOR THE SURVIVING ENTITY DATE	TYPE OR PRINT NAME AND TITLE OF AUTHORIZED PERSON
SIGNATURE OF AUTHORIZED PERSON FOR THE SURVIVING ENTITY DATE	TYPE OR PRINT NAME AND TITLE OF AUTHORIZED PERSON
SIGNATURE OF AUTHORIZED PERSON FOR THE DISAPPEARING ENTITY DATE	TYPE OR PRINT NAME AND TITLE OF AUTHORIZED PERSON
SIGNATURE OF AUTHORIZED PERSON FOR THE DISAPPEARING ENTITY DATE	TYPE OR PRINT NAME AND TITLE OF AUTHORIZED PERSON

For an entity that is a business trust, real estate investment trust or an unincorporated association, set forth the provision of law or other basis for the authority of the person signing:_______________________________

OBE MERGER-1 (REV 01/2016) APPROVED BY SECRETARY OF STATE

DOCUMENT SIX

Certificate of Dissolution

CA FORM: DISS STK

http://bpd.cdn.sos.ca.gov/corp/pdf/dissolutions/corp_stkdiss.pdf

"DISS STK: Domestic Stock Corporation Certificate of Dissolution," https://bpd.cdn.sos.ca.gov/corp/pdf/dissolutions/corp_stkdiss.pdf, State of California, 2019.

(*Continued*)

DISS STK

Secretary of State
Certificate of Dissolution

(California Stock Corporation ONLY)

IMPORTANT—Read Instructions before completing this form.

There is **No Fee** for filing a Certificate of Dissolution—Stock

Copy Fees—First page $1.00; each attachment page $0.50;
Certification Fee—$5.00 plus copy fees

This Space For Office Use Only

1. Corporate Name (Enter the exact name of the Corporation as it is recorded with the California Secretary of State.)	**2. 7-Digit Secretary of State File Number**

3. Election

☐ The dissolution was made by a vote of **ALL** of the shareholders of the California corporation.
Note: If the above box is not checked, a **Certificate of Election to Wind Up and Dissolve** (Form ELEC STK) must be filed prior to or together with this Certificate of Dissolution. (California Corporations Code section 1901.)

4. Debts and Liabilities (Check the applicable statement. Only **one box** may be checked. If second box is checked, must include the required information in an attachment.)

☐ The known debts and liabilities have been actually paid or paid as far as its assets permitted.
☐ The known debts and liabilities have been adequately provided for in full or as far as its assets permitted by their assumption. Included in the **attachment** to this certificate, incorporated herein by this reference, is a description of the provisions made and the name and address of the person, corporation or government agency that has assumed or guaranteed the payment, or the depository institution with which deposit has been made.
☐ The corporation never incurred any known debts or liabilities.

5. Required Statements (Do not alter the Required Statements - **ALL** must be true to file Form DISS STK.)

a. The Corporation has been completely wound up and is dissolved.
b. All final returns required under the California Revenue and Taxation Code have been or will be filed with the California Franchise Tax Board.
c. The known assets have been distributed to the persons entitled thereto or the corporation acquired no known assets.

6. Read, Verify, Date and Sign Below (See Instructions for signature requirements.)

The undersigned is the sole director or a majority of the directors now in office. I declare under penalty of perjury under the laws of the State of California that the matters set forth in this certificate are true and correct of my own knowledge.

Date	Signature	Type or Print Name
Date	Signature	Type or Print Name
Date	Signature	Type or Print Name

DISS STK (REV 07/2019)

2019 California Secretary of State
bizfile.sos.ca.gov

SECTION II

General Partnerships

DOCUMENT SEVEN

Partnership Agreement (EPCOR Power GP)

S-4 2012-05-18 EX-3.60

https://www.sec.gov/Archives/edgar/data/1419242/000104746912006170/a2206677zex-3_60.htm

AMENDED AND RESTATED PARTNERSHIP AGREEMENT OF EPCOR POWER (US) GP

Dated As of July 20, 2007
between
EPCOR POWER EQUITY LTD.
and
EPLP POWER INC.

TABLE OF CONTENTS

"Amended and Restated Partnership Agreement of Epcor Power (US) GP," https://www.sec.gov/Archives/edgar/data/1419242/000104746912006170/a2206677zex-3_60.htm, U.S. Securities and Exchange Commission, 2007.

Partnership Agreement of EPCOR Power (US) GP

THIS AMENDED AND RESTATED PARTNERSHIP AGREEMENT (this "Agreement") of EPCOR Power (US) GP, a Delaware partnership (the "Partnership"), is made and entered into effective as of July 20, 2007 (the "Effective Date") by and between EPCOR POWER EQUITY LTD., an Alberta corporation ("EPEL"), and EPLP POWER INC., an Alberta corporation ("EPLPPI", and together with EPEL, sometimes hereinafter collectively referred to as the "Partners"), amending and restating, in its entirety, the Partnership Agreement dated as of June 1, 2007 between EPEL and EPCOR POWER (WILLIAMS LAKE) LTD., a British Columbia corporation ("EPWLL") (the "Initial Agreement"), with reference to the following facts:

A. The Partnership was formed for the purpose of carrying on in common, with a view to profit, the business of acquiring, owning, operating, managing, financing, selling or otherwise disposing of and liquidating subsidiaries engaged in the acquisition, development, construction, commissioning, ownership, management, operation, maintenance, financing, sale, disposition, decommissioning and liquidation of electric generating facilities, combined heat and power facilities and other facilities in the United States, and undertaking any and all activities related and incidental to any of the foregoing, and earning and sharing profits and losses from such business, all as more specifically hereinafter set forth;
B. Pursuant to the Assignment and Assumption Agreement (as defined below), EPLPPI has purchased from EPWLL the 0.5 percent Partnership Interest held by EPWLL in the Partnership; and
C. The Partners desire to continue the Partnership and to amend and restate in its entirety the Initial Agreement in the form hereof.

In consideration of the mutual covenants contained herein, and other valuable consideration, the receipt and sufficiency of which are hereby acknowledged, the parties, intending to be legally bound, hereby agree, and hereby enter into this Agreement in its entirety, as follows:

ARTICLE I: RULES OF CONSTRUCTION; DEFINITIONS

Section 1.1 Rules of Construction. For purposes hereof, capitalized terms used herein shall have the meanings assigned to such terms in this Article I. Unless otherwise indicated, references to the masculine shall be deemed to include the feminine, references to the singular shall be deemed to include the plural, and references to "or" shall be deemed to be disjunctive but not necessarily exclusive. Any agreement defined or referred to below shall include each amendment, modification and supplement thereto, and each waiver, approval and consent in respect thereof, as may become effective from time to time, except where otherwise indicated, and shall include all Appendices, Exhibits, Schedules and other attachments thereto and instruments, agreements or other documents incorporated therein. Any term defined below by reference to any document shall be deemed to be amended herein to the extent that such term is subsequently amended in such document. If any such document is subsequently amended, modified or terminated, the affected parties to this Agreement shall in good faith select another comparable definition for any term theretofore defined below by reference to such document.

Unless the context otherwise requires: any reference to any statute, law or governmental regulation will include all amendments, modifications and successors thereto and any replacements of the specific sections and provisions concerned; a reference to any Person includes its successors and assigns; accounting terms not otherwise defined have the meanings assigned to them by GAAP applied on a consistent basis by the accounting entity to which they refer; unless otherwise indicated, all references to Sections, other subdivisions, Appendices, Schedules and Exhibits shall mean and refer to the respective Sections, other subdivisions, Appendices, Schedules and Exhibits in or attached to the agreement or document in which such reference appears; the words "include", "includes" and "including" are not limiting and shall be deemed to be followed by the words "without limitation" whether or not in fact followed by such words or words of like import; and the terms "hereof", "herein", "hereunder" and comparable terms refer to the entire agreement with respect to which such terms are used and not to any particular article, section or other subdivision thereof.

No provision of this Agreement shall be construed in favor of or against either of the parties hereto by reason of the extent to which any such party or its counsel participated in the drafting thereof or by reason of the extent to which such provision or any other provision or provisions of this Agreement is or are inconsistent with any prior draft thereof.

Section 1.2 Certain Defined Terms. As used in this Agreement, the following terms shall have the following meanings:

"Affiliate" means with respect to any Person, any other Person who, directly or indirectly, Controls such first Person or is Controlled by said Person or is under common Control with said Person.

"Agreement" means this Partnership Agreement as originally executed and as amended from time to time.

"Approval of the Partners" means approval by the affirmative vote of the Partner(s) holding a majority (in percentage terms) of the Partner Percentage Interests.

"Assignment and Assumption Agreement" means the Assignment and Assumption Agreement dated as of July 20, 2007 by and between EPLPPI and EPWLL.

"Business Day" shall mean any day other than Saturday, Sunday or any other day on which commercial banks are required or permitted to close by law in The City of New York.

"Capital Contribution" means the amount of money and the agreed Fair Market Value of other property (net of any liabilities secured by such property that the Partnership is considered to assume or take subject to under Code Section 752) contributed by a Partner to the Partnership pursuant to this Agreement.

"Code" means the Internal Revenue Code of 1986, as amended from time to time.

"Composite Taxes" shall mean any taxes assessed against or customarily paid by the Partnership.

"Contract" means any agreement, security agreement, indenture, contract, lease, deed of trust, license, option, instrument or other commitment, whether written or oral.

"Control" means the possession, directly or indirectly, through one or more intermediaries, of both of the following:

(a) in the case of a corporation, the ownership of a majority of the outstanding equity and voting securities thereof; in the case of a limited liability company, partnership, limited partnership or joint venture, the ownership right to a majority of the distributions therefrom (including liquidating distributions); in the case of a trust or estate, including a business trust, the ownership of a majority of the beneficial interest thereof; and in the case of any other entity or organization, the ownership of a majority of the economic or beneficial interest therein; and

(b) the power and authority, through the ownership or control of voting rights or by Contract or otherwise, to direct or cause the direction of the management of such corporation, limited liability company, partnership, limited partnership, joint venture, trust, estate or other entity or organization and "Controls", "Controlled by" and "under common Control with" have corresponding meanings.

"Distributable Cash" shall mean, as of any date, the cash funds and cash equivalents of the Partnership as of such date that the Partners determine are not required to be retained by the Partnership:

(a) to meet the then projected cash requirements and needs of the Partnership for the next six months in accordance with the budget of the Partnership, taking into account a reasonable estimate of revenues to be received during such period;
(b) to pay Composite Taxes and other assessments chargeable, if any, payable by the Partnership during the next six months;
(c) to pay and discharge any current liabilities and obligations of the Partnership as the same become due and payable during the next six months, including scheduled principal and interest on indebtedness for borrowed money, as well as any additional amounts that may be required to be paid under or in respect of such indebtedness during the next six months; and
(d) to maintain a cash reserve in an amount determined by the Partners for cash disbursements, including a provision for the payment of all outstanding and unpaid current obligations of the Partnership as well as any capital expenditures which, in the determination of the Partners may be required, in each case during the next six months.

"Effective Date" means the date first set forth above.

"Encumbrance" means any encumbrance, lien, charge, hypothec, pledge, mortgage, title retention agreement, security interest or third party interest of any nature, adverse claim, exception, reservation, easement, right of occupation, any matter capable of registration against title, option, right of first refusal, right of pre-emption, privilege or any Contract to create any of the foregoing, but does not include Permitted Encumbrances.

"Fair Market Value" means, in relation to any property, the highest price available in an open and unrestricted market between informed and prudent parties, acting at arm's length and under no compulsion to act, expressed in terms of money or money's worth.

"GAAP" means United States generally accepted accounting principles as in effect from time to time.

"Governmental Approval" means any consent, approval or authorization of, or declaration, filing or registration with, or notice to, or order or action of, any court, administrative agency or other Governmental Authority.

"Governmental Authority" means any federal, provincial, state, local, foreign, municipal, quasi-municipal or other governmental authority, including a state, province, commonwealth, country, territory or district thereof; any city, town, township, village or other municipality; any district, ward or other subdivision of any of the foregoing; any executive, legislative or other governing body of any of the foregoing; any agency, authority, board, department, system, service, office, commission, committee, council or other administrative body of any of the foregoing; any court or other judicial body; and any officer, official or other representative of any of the foregoing.

"Initial Agreement" has the meaning set forth in the first paragraph of this Agreement.

"Insolvency Event" means, as to any partner, that:

(a) such Partner makes an assignment of property for the benefit of creditors, or a sheriff, receiver, trustee or conservator seizes any material portion of the assets of such Partner;
(b) a monitor, receiver, conservator, liquidator or trustee in bankruptcy is appointed in respect of such Partner, its Partnership Interest or any material portion of its assets;
(c) any proceeding relating to a compromise or arrangement with such Partner's creditors is commenced under bankruptcy or insolvency Laws, or Laws for relief of debtors, including the filing of a voluntary or involuntary petition under federal bankruptcy Law, unless such proceeding is disputed by the Partner in good faith and is dismissed within 30 days after it is commenced;
(d) such Partner is adjudged or declared bankrupt or insolvent under applicable bankruptcy or insolvency legislation;
(e) such Partner admits in writing that it is bankrupt, insolvent or unable to pay its debts as they become due; or
(f) such Partner defaults under any agreement or instrument which renders enforceable an Encumbrance on its Partnership Interest and such default is not cured within the cure period (if any) permitted by such agreement or instrument.

"Internal Costs" means, in relation to a Partner and without duplication, (a) the normal salaries, wages and employee benefits of the employees of such Partner and its Affiliates that are attributable to the time that such employees expend in respect of Partnership Activities, (b) reasonable transportation, accommodation and similar out of pocket costs of such employees which are incurred in connection with Partnership Activities, and (c) a reasonable amount on account of the general and administrative overhead expenses of such Partner and its Affiliates that are attributable to the costs described in (a) and (b) above and other Partnership Activities undertaken by such Partner and its Affiliates. A Partner's Internal Costs shall be calculated on the basis that such Partner shall not earn a profit or suffer a loss in respect of its Internal Costs. A Partner's Internal Costs will not include its costs of capital or its interest costs.

"Law" means all statutes, regulations, ordinances, rules, orders, common law legal and equitable principles, codes of federal, provincial, state, local and foreign Governmental Authorities, and includes any order, decree, ruling, proclamation, resolution, judgment, decision or declaration of a Governmental Authority having valid jurisdiction, all as may be amended from time to time.

"Net Income" or "Net Loss", as appropriate, shall mean, for any period, the income or loss of the Partnership from each source and activity of the Partnership for such period, as determined in accordance with GAAP.

"Non-Resident" means a Person that is not a resident of Canada within the meaning of the Tax Act and includes a partnership that is not a "Canadian Partnership" as defined in the Tax Act.

"Order" means any writ, judgment, decree, injunction or similar order of any arbitrator or any court, tribunal or other Governmental Authority having jurisdiction (in each case whether preliminary or final).

"Partner" means a partner of the Partnership.

"Partner Percentage Interest" means, with respect to each Partner, the percentage Partnership Interest of such Partner, expressed as a percentage of the total Partnership Interests, as set forth on Exhibit B hereto opposite such Partner's name, as amended from time to time.

"Partnership" means EPCOR Power (US) GP, a Delaware partnership.

"Partnership Act" means the Revised Uniform Partnership Act of the State of Delaware, as amended.

"Partnership Activities" means activities required to be carried out for the benefit of the Partnership in connection with the conduct and operation of its business activities.

"Partnership Interest" means an interest of a Partner in the Partnership, including rights to share in Net Income, Net Losses, Taxable Income and Tax Loss, rights to distributions, and rights and obligations under this Agreement and the Partnership Act.

"Person" means any individual, corporation, partnership, limited liability company, firm, association, trust, Governmental Authority, unincorporated organization or any other entity, in each case whether acting in an individual, fiduciary or other capacity.

"Tax" includes all Canadian federal, provincial, territorial or municipal and all United States federal, state, local and all foreign or other taxes, rates, levies, assessments, charges and duties, including taxes measured on income and on gains derived from dispositions of property; sale, excise, capital, business transfer and value added taxes; taxes measured on capital or assets used in a business; customs and impart and export duties; and interest, penalties and fines levied or assessed in respect of any of the foregoing.

"Tax Act" means the *Income Tax Act* (Canada), together with all regulations made pursuant thereto, as amended from time to time.

"Taxable Income" or "Tax Loss" means the amount of income or loss of the Partnership for a Fiscal Year determined pursuant to the provisions of the Tax Act.

"Transfer" means any transfer, assignment, conveyance, sale encumbrance, grant of any lien or security interest in, mortgage, pledge, hypothecation or any other alienations of, or change in the record or beneficial ownership of, a Partnership Interest, including any transfer that would result in any Partner ceasing to own its Partnership Interest, whether made voluntarily or involuntarily by operation of law.

"Transferee Partner" means an additional Partner admitted to the Partnership in accordance with the terms of this Agreement upon Transfer of an existing Partner's Partnership Interest.

"Treasury Regulations" shall mean the regulations promulgated by the U.S. Department of the Treasury under the Code.

ARTICLE II: ORGANIZATIONAL MATTERS

Section 2.1 Formation. The Partners agree to continue the Partnership as a partnership under and pursuant to the provisions of the Partnership Act and agree that the rights, duties and liabilities of the Partners shall be as provided in the Partnership Act, except as otherwise provided herein. This Agreement shall become binding and effective as an agreement among the Partners as of the Effective Date.

Section 2.2 Name. The name of the Partnership in EPCOR Power (US) GP.

Section 2.3 Principal Place of Business. The principal place of business of the Partnership will be located within the United States, at any place or places as the Partners may from time to time deem advisable. The books and records of the Partnership shall be maintained at its principal place of business and shall be available to each Partner for inspection and copying.

Section 2.4 Partnership Property. All property and rights and interests in property originally brought into the Partnership or acquired, whether by purchase or otherwise, on account of the Partnership, or for the purposes and in the cause of the Partnership business, will be held and applied by the Partnership exclusively for the purposes of the Partnership and in accordance with this Agreement.

Section 2.5 Term. The term of the Partnership shall commence on June 1, 2007 and shall continue until the earlier of January 1, 2050 or the dissolution of the Partnership as provided in Section 8.1.

Section 2.6 Fiscal Year. The Partnership's annual accounting period (the "Fiscal Year") shall be a calendar year.

Section 2.7 Names and Addresses of Partners. The name and address of the Partners are set forth on Exhibit A attached hereto. The Partners shall cause Exhibit A to be updated from time to time as necessary to reflect accurately the information therein. Any amendment or revision to Exhibit A made in accordance with this Agreement shall not be deemed an amendment to this Agreement. Any reference in this Agreement to Exhibit A shall be deemed to be a reference to Exhibit A as amended or restated, and in effect from time to time.

Section 2.8 Liability of Partners. The Partners shall have unlimited liability for the payment, satisfaction and discharge of all debts, liabilities and obligations of the Partnership to the full extent of its assets.

Section 2.9 New Partners. Except as expressly permitted by Article VII, no new Partners shall be admitted to the Partnership except with the written consent of all of the Partners, and in no event shall any Person that is a Non-Resident be admitted as a Partner in the Partnership.

Section 2.10 Qualification in Other Jurisdictions. The Partners shall cause the Partnership to be qualified, formed or registered under assumed or fictitious name statutes or similar Laws in any jurisdiction in which the Partnership transacts business. Each Partner shall execute, deliver and file any certificates (and any amendments or restatements thereof) which the Partners may deem necessary or advisable in order for the Partnership to qualify to do business in any jurisdiction in which the Partnership may wish to conduct business.

Section 2.11 Agent for Service of Process. The agent for service of process on the Partnership in the State of Delaware is The Corporation Trust Company and the mailing address for the registered office of the Company in the State of Delaware is in care of The Corporation Trust Company, 1209 Orange Street, Wilmington, Delaware 19801. Such agent and such office may be changed from time to time by the Partners.

Section 2.12 Representation and Warranty of Partners. Each Partner represents, warrants and covenants to each and every other Partner that it is not and will not be a Non-Resident for so long as it is a Partner, and that it will not knowingly transfer its Partnership Interest to any Person that is a Non-Resident.

Section 2.13 Partnership Not Separate Legal Entity. Pursuant to Section 15-201(a) of the Partnership Act, the Partners agree that the Partnership shall not constitute a separate legal entity distinct from the Partners and will stipulate as such in the Statement of Partnership Existence filed with the Secretary of State of the State of Delaware.

ARTICLE III: BUSINESS OF THE PARTNERSHIP

Section 3.1 Business. The business of the Partnership shall be that of acquiring, owing, operating, managing, financing, selling or otherwise disposing of and liquidating subsidiaries engaged in the acquisition, development, construction, commissioning, ownership, management, operation, maintenance, financing, sale, disposition, decommissioning and liquidation of electric generating facilities, combined heat and power facilities and other facilities in the United States, and undertaking any and all activities related and incidental to any of the foregoing. Any deviation from the Partnership's stated purposes shall require the Approval of the Partners. The Partners shall devote such time and attention to the business of the Partnership as is reasonably necessary to the conduct of such business and shall act as mutual agents of each other in their relationship as Partners.

Section 3.2 Borrowing. Without in any way limiting the provisions of Section 3.1, the Partnership shall have the right, power and authority to borrow money on a secured or unsecured basis from individuals, banks and other lending institutions in order to finance or refinance Partnership assets, meet other Partnership obligations, provide Partnership working capital and for any other Partnership purpose, and to execute promissory notes, mortgages, deeds of trust and assignments of Partnership property and such other security instruments as a lender of funds may require to secure repayment of such borrowing.

ARTICLE IV: PARTNERSHIP INTERESTS

Section 4.1 Capital Contributions of the Partners. As of the date of this Agreement, each Partner has contributed to the Partnership the consideration set forth opposite its name on Exhibit B hereto in the form indicated thereon (each such contribution, a "Capital Contribution"). The agreed value of the Capital Contributions is as set forth on Exhibit B. Each Partner has, in consideration for its Capital Contribution, received the Partner Percentage Interest set forth opposite its name on Exhibit B hereto.

Section 4.2 Further Issuances. Following the execution and delivery of this Agreement, the Partnership may issue other Partnership Interests and admit the purchasers thereof as Partners as authorized and consented to by the Partners from time to time with such rights as the Partners may determine. Upon the issuance of additional Partnership Interests, each Partner's Partner Percentage Interest shall be adjusted downward to accurately reflect the appropriate percentage of dilution.

Section 4.3 Additional Capital Contributions. No Partner shall be required to make any Capital Contribution to the Partnership after the date of this Agreement except as agreed by the Partners. No voluntary Capital Contribution by any Partner other than the Capital Contributions shall be permitted unless otherwise agreed to by the Partners. Upon a Partner making any additional Capital Contribution, Exhibit B hereto shall be amended as appropriate to reflect the revised Partner Percentage Interest of each Partner.

Section 4.4 Claims of Partners. The Partners shall have no right to the return of their Capital Contributions, if any, other than as specifically provided herein and shall have no recourse against the Partnership or any Partner for the return of such amount, other than as specifically provided herein. Upon any return to any Partner of any Capital Contribution or portion thereof, Exhibit B hereto shall be amended as appropriate to reflect the revised Partner Percentage Interest of each Partner.

ARTICLE V: DISTRIBUTIONS AND ALLOCATIONS

Section 5.1 Allocations of Net Income and Net Loss.

(a) For each Fiscal Year, or any portion thereof with respect to which the provisions of this Agreement require allocations to be made, Net Income and Net Loss shall be allocated to the Partners in proportion to their respective Partner Percentage Interests.

(b) For purposes of the foregoing allocation provisions of this Section 5.1, in the event of any Transfers, issuances, redemptions or forfeitures of Partnership Interests or other changes in the proportionate holdings of Partnership Interests during a Fiscal Year, Net Income and Net Loss for the Fiscal Year shall be allocated to the Partners holding Partnership Interests immediately before such event and the Partners holding Partnership Interests immediately after such event, respectively, based on an interim closing of the books and, with respect to the period ending immediately before such event and the period beginning at the time of such event, shall otherwise be allocated among Partners in accordance with the allocation provisions of this Section 5.1.

(c) All matters concerning allocations, designations, elections and income computation for United States or Canadian federal, provincial, state and local and foreign income tax purposes, including accounting procedures, not expressly provided for by the terms of this Agreement shall be determined by the Approval of the Partners.

Section 5.2 Allocations of Taxable Income or Tax Loss.

(a) Subject to Sections 5.2(b), 5.2(c) and 5.2(d), Taxable Income or Tax Loss of the Partnership from each source and activity of the Partnership and each taxable capital gain and allowable capital loss of the Partnership from the disposition of property in respect of a Fiscal Year will be allocated to the Partners in proportion to their respective Partner Percentage Interests.

(b) Where assets of the Partnership which were originally contributed to the Partnership by a Partner on a "rollover" or other tax deferred basis are subsequently disposed of by the Partnership, then for the purposes of computing the Taxable Income, Tax Loss, capital gain or capital loss of such Partner under the Tax Act or any statute of any province or territory of Canada imposing a tax on income, an amount of income or gain which is attributable to the difference between the fair market value of such assets at the time of their contribution to the Partnership and the Partnership's tax basis therein at such time shall be allocated to the Partner who so contributed such assets.

(c) Where assets of the Partnership are distributed in kind to a Partner and the distribution results in Taxable Income, Tax Loss, capital gain or capital loss to the Partnership, then for the purposes of computing the Taxable Income, Tax Loss, capital gain or capital loss of a

Partner under the Tax Act or any statute of any province or territory of Canada imposing a tax on income, such income or gain or loss shall be allocated to the Partner receiving such distribution.

(d) In the event of any Transfers, issuances, redemptions or forfeitures of Partnership Interests or other changes in the proportionate holdings of Partnership Interests during a Fiscal Year, Taxable Income and Tax Loss for the Fiscal Year shall be allocated to the Partners holding Partnership Interests immediately before such event and the Partners holding Partnership Interests immediately after such event, respectively, based on an interim Fiscal Year end at the time of such event, and, with respect to the period ending immediately before such event and the period beginning at the time of such event, shall otherwise be allocated among Partners in accordance with the allocation provisions of this Section 5.2.

Section 5.3 Cash Distributions. The Partnership shall make distributions of Distributable Cash, at such time or times as may be determined by the Approval of the Partners, in proportion to the Partners' respective Partner Percentage Interests at the time of such distribution.

Section 5.4 General Limitation. Notwithstanding any provision to the contrary in this Agreement, the Partnership shall not make any distributions except to the extent permitted under the Partnership Act.

Section 5.5 Distributions in Kind. All distributions under this Article V shall be in cash unless the Partners determine, by the Approval of the Partners, to make such distributions in whole or in part in kind (in which case such distributions in kind shall be made pro rata in accordance with the total amounts to be distributed to the Partners). For purposes of this Agreement, including for purpose of determining amounts distributable to any Partner under Section 5.4 and for purposes of the allocation under Article V, any property to be distributed in kind shall be assigned its Fair Market Value in such manner as may be reasonably determined by the Partners, such determination shall be conclusive and binding on all Partners, and such Fair Market Value shall be treated for all purposes hereof as a like amount of cash.

Section 5.6 Set Off and Withholding. Notwithstanding any provision to the contrary in this Agreement, the Partners may cause the Partnership to set off against, or withhold from, any distribution of cash or property in kind to any Partner, in respect of any amounts due from such Partner to the Partnership under this Agreement, to the extent not otherwise paid. Any amounts so set off or withheld shall be applied by the Partnership to discharge the obligation in respect of which such amounts were set off or withheld. All amounts set off or withheld under this Section 5.6 that are attributable to any Partner shall be treated as amounts distributed to such Partner for all purposes under this Agreement.

ARTICLE VI: MANAGEMENT AND ADMINISTRATION OF THE PARTNERSHIP; TAX MATTERS

Section 6.1 Management of the Partnership; Voting Rights.

(a) Notwithstanding anything to the contrary in this Agreement or in the Partnership Act (other than provisions thereof that specifically cannot be altered by the Partners), each Partner shall be entitled to vote on any action or matter as to which the partners of a general partnership are granted voting rights pursuant to the provisions of the Partners Act or as to which the Partners are expressly granted voting rights pursuant to the provisions of this Agreement. Without limiting the foregoing, each Partner shall be entitled to vote on any action or matter relating to the manner of exercise of voting or other shareholder or ownership rights with respect to shares or other interests that the Partnership holds in other entities. In connection therewith, each Partner shall have a vote equivalent to the Partner Percentage Interest of such Partner at such time. Partnership action on all matters shall be approved if the votes cast in favor of the action exceed the votes cast in opposition to such action, other than:

(i) as required by the Partnership Act or other applicable Law;
(ii) those decisions under which a Partner will incur personal liability or obligations, including obligations to contribute capital to the Partnership or provide credit support or other financial assistance to the Partnership, provided that, each Partner will be obligated to provide the Partnership (by Capital Contribution) its Partner Percentage Interest share of all costs of business activities approved by the Partners, to the extent that the Partnership does not have available funds to pay such costs; and
(iii) a decision to delegate to one Person (other than EPEL) all of the Partners' power to manage, control, administer and operate the affairs of the Partnership.

(b) Any vote or consent of the Partners may be given by written ballot or by vote at a meeting of the Partners called for that purpose or by written consent without a meeting. EPEL may at any time call a meeting of the Partners or call for a vote of the Partners without a meeting on matters on which they are entitled to vote or consent. EPEL shall call for such a meeting or vote following receipt of a written request from any Partner. Within 10 days after receipt of any such notice, EPEL shall notify all affected Partners of record as of the notice date regarding the time and place of the Partnership meeting and the general nature of the business to be transacted at the meeting. Any Partnership meeting shall be not less that 15 days or more than 60 days following mailing of the meeting notice by EPEL.

Section 6.2 Income Tax Matters; Designated Member. EPEL is hereby authorized to act on behalf of the Partnership and each of its Partners in connection with any determination that may be made by the Canada Revenue Agency and any provincial or territorial taxing authority in Canada pursuant to the provisions of Section 152(1.4) of the Tax Act, as the same may be amended, and any analogous Canadian provincial or territorial legislation; and for greater certainty, EPEL is hereby appointed the designated member of the Partnership and is hereby authorized by the Partnership and each of its Partners to make an objection in respect of any such determination.

Section 6.3 Indemnification of Third Parties. The Partnership shall indemnify each person (other than a Partner) engaged in the management, administration or operation of the business and affairs of the Partnership as a representative of the Partners or any other committee established by the Partners or as an employee of the Partnership to the fullest extent permitted by applicable Law, provided that no such Person shall be entitled to indemnification in respect of willfull misconduct, gross negligence, or an act or omission not taken in good faith or which the Person had reasonable cause to believe was unlawful. The Parties agree that the provisions of the Section 6.3 are not appropriate for Contracts for the provision of goods or services to the Partnership and that such Contracts shall incorporate such standards of care as the Partners consider appropriate and in accordance with industry standards.

ARTICLE VII: RESTRICTIONS ON TRANSFER OF PARTNERSHIP INTERESTS

Section 7.1 Permitted Transfers of Partnership Interests. No Partner may at any time, on from time to time, Transfer all or any portion of its Partnership Interest to a Person that is not an Affiliate of such Transferring Partner without obtaining (a) the prior written and unanimous approval of the other Partner(s) (which approval may be given or withheld, conditioned or delayed by each such other Partner in its sole and absolute discretion) and (b) all necessary Government Approvals; provided, however, that, subject to compliance with Section 7.3, any Partner may Transfer all or any portion of its Partnership Interest to an Affiliate upon obtaining (x) the prior approval of the Partner(s) holding a majority of the Partner Percentage Interests not held by the Transferring Partner and (y) all necessary Government Approvals. After the consummation of any Transfer of all or any part of a Partnership Interest, the Partnership Interest so Transferred shall continue to be subject to the terms and provisions of this Agreement and any further Transfers shall be required to comply with all the terms and provisions of this Agreement. Notwithstanding the foregoing, in no event may a Partner Transfer all or any portion of its Partnership Interest to a Non-Resident.

Section 7.2 Effective Date of Permitted Transfers. Any permitted Transfer of all or any portion of a Partnership Interest shall be effective as of the date upon which each and all of the requirements of Section 7.1 have been met. Any Transferee of a Partnership Interest shall take such Partnership Interest subject to the restrictions on Transfer imposed by this Agreement.

Section 7.3 Rights of First Offer. Except as provided in Section 7.3(a) below, no Partner shall effect in whole or in part any Transfer of a Partnership Interest to any Person unless such Partner first complies with the first offer procedures described in Section 7.3(a) below (the "Partner First Offer Rights"). The Partner First Offer Rights shall be as follows:

(a) If any Partner at any time desires to effect a Transfer of all or any portion of its Partnership Interest(s), such Partner shall first give a notice (a "Partner Offer Notice") to the other Partners (the "Partner Offerees"), offering to sell such Partnership Interest (the "Partner Offered Interest") to the Partner Offerees at the price and on the other terms and conditions set forth in such Partner Offer Notice. The Partner Offerees shall have the right, for a period of 30 days after receipt of such Partner Offer Notice (the "Partner Offer Period"), to elect to purchase from such Partner all (but not less than all) of the Partner Offered Interest at the purchase price and on the other terms and conditions specified in the Partner Offered Notice by giving such Partner notice of such Election (a "Partner Exercise Notice"). If more than one Partner Offeree makes such election, the percentage of such Partner Offered Interest that each electing Partner Offeree (the "Electing Partner Offerees") shall be entitled to purchase shall be determined on a pro rata basis in proportion to their respective Partner Percentage Interests. Such Partner Exercise Notice may be given separately or jointly by more than on Electing Partner Offeree. In any such Partner Exercise Notice, the Electing Partner Offeree may specify that the Partner Offered Interest will be purchased by such Electing Partner Offeree or one or more of its respective Affiliates. Upon the giving of a valid Partner Exercise Notice, the parties shall cause the Partner Offered Interest to be sold to the purchaser(s) specified therein in accordance with the terms and conditions specified in the applicable Partner Offer Notice and the sale procedures described in Section 7.3(c).

(b) If none of the Partner Offerees give such Partner a Partner Exercise Notice within the Partner Offer Period, then at any time within 90 days commencing upon the expiration of such Partner Offer Period, such Partner may enter into a binding agreement to Transfer all (but not less than all) of the Partner Offered Interest to any Person, subject to the Transfer restrictions set forth in Section 7.1 (to the extent applicable). If consummation of such Transfer is not precluded pursuant to such Transfer restrictions, such Partner may proceed to close such Transfer, which closing shall (i) occur no later than 90 days after the expiration of such 90 day period, (ii) be at a price not less than the price set forth in the Partner Offer Notice, and (iii) be on terms and conditions substantially the same as those specified in the Partner Offer Notice. The time periods specified in the Section 7.3(b) shall be extended to the extent necessary to accommodate any required Governmental Authority filings or Governmental Approvals, each of which filings and approvals such Partner agrees to use its best efforts to make or obtain as quickly as reasonably practicable. If such Partner fails to agree to and close a permitted Transfer within the above specified periods, then all of the restrictions stated in the Section 7.3 shall apply again as though no Partner Offer Notice had been hereunder.

(c) The closing of any purchase by a Partner (or its Affiliate) of a Partner Offered Interest hereunder shall take place at a time and place reasonably acceptable to the participating parties. Prior to any such closing, the parties shall take all other actions required to permit such closing to take place, including, without limitation, making any required filings with Governmental Authorities, obtaining any required Governmental Approvals and obtaining any required contractual consents. At such closing, the Transferor of any Partnership Interest shall deliver to the applicable purchaser(s) such documentation as such purchaser(s) may reasonably request to evidence the Transfer of such interest against payment of the purchase price therefor.

(d) The Partner First Offer Rights shall not apply to any Transfer from a Partner to its Affiliate; provided, that, in the case of Transfers to a Affiliate, the Transferee(s) agree in writing in a form reasonably satisfactory to the parties to this Agreement to be bound by each of the provisions of this Agreement in respect of the Transferred interest(s).

Section 7.4 Admission of Transferee as Partner. A Transferee of a Partnership Interest, including an Affiliate of a Partner desiring to be admitted as a Partner, must execute a counterpart of, or an agreement adopting, this Agreement and any and all relevant related agreements as the Partnership may reasonably require. Subject to obtaining the foregoing required consents, if applicable, and compliance with the applicable provisions of this Agreement, a Transferee of a Partnership Interest shall be admitted as Partner. Upon the admission of the Transferee as a Partner, the Transferee shall have, to the extent of the Partnership Interest Transferred, the rights and powers and shall be subject to the restrictions and liabilities of a Partner under this Agreement and the Partnership Act. The Transferee shall also be liable, to the extent of the Partnership Interest Transferred, for the unfulfilled obligations, if any, of the Transferor Partner to make Capital Contributions, but shall not be obligated for liabilities unknown to the Transferee at the time such Transferee was admitted as a Partner and that could not be ascertained from this Agreement. Except as otherwise provided in this Agreement, and except with respect to liabilities unknown to the Transferee at the time of the Transfer and that could not be ascertained from this Agreement, upon admission of such Transferee as a Partner, the Transferor Partner shall be released from any liability to the Partnership under this Agreement and the Partnership Act.

Section 7.5 Transfers in Violation of Agreement.

(a) Except as hereinafter expressly provided, any attempted Transfer of a Partnership Interest in violation of the foregoing restrictions, and any attempted charge upon or attachment of a Partnership Interest by judicial process, a foreclosure by a creditor of a Partner or otherwise, shall be invalid, null and void and of no force or effect whatsoever, and no Person shall as a result of any such attempted Transfer, charge or attachment acquire or succeed to any rights or interests associated with such Partnership Interest, including but not limited to any right to vote or participate in the management of the Partnership, property and affairs of the Partnership, receive any share of the Partnership's Net Income, Net Loss or distributions of the Partnership's assets or exercise any other rights of a Partner.

(b) Upon any attempted Transfer of a Partnership Interest in violation of the foregoing restrictions, and any attempted charge upon or attachment of a Partner's Partnership interest by judicial process, a foreclosure by a creditor of a Partner or otherwise, the Transferee shall have no right to vote or participate in the management of the business, property and affairs of the Partnership or to exercise any rights of a Partner, including, without limitation, the right to vote or participate in the management of the Partnership, or, except as otherwise expressly provided by Law, any right to information concerning the business and affairs of the Partnership.

(c) Except to the extent otherwise expressly agreed, no purchase and sale of a Partner's Partnership Interest pursuant to this Article VII shall result in the release of the Partner from any liability incurred by the Partner to the Partnership or any other Partner prior to the closing of such purchase and sale.

Section 7.6 Adjustment of Partner Percentage Interests. The Partner Percentage Interests of the Partners shall be adjusted as appropriate to reflect any permitted Transfer of any Transferring Partner's Partnership Interest under this Article.

ARTICLE VIII: DISSOLUTION AND TERMINATION OF THE PARTNERSHIP

Section 8.1 Dissolution and Termination of the Partnership. Any decision to wind up the business and affairs of the Partnership or to dispose of all or substantially all of the assets of the Partnership requires the Approval of the Partners. In the event dissolution of the Partnership is approved, distributions to the Partners shall be made at the same time or times and in proportion to their respective Partner Percentage Interests. Distributions may be effected in kind if the Approval of the Partners has been obtained, any such distributions shall be effected, to the extent practicable, in a manner that defers, to the maximum extent possible, taxes that would otherwise be payable by the Partnership or the Partners.

ARTICLE IX: MISCELLANEOUS PROVISIONS

Section 9.1 Notices.

(a) Notice Methods and Addresses. All notices, requests, demands and other communications required or permitted to be given hereunder shall be given in writing (i) by personal delivery, (ii) by recognized overnight air courier service, (iii) by United States or Canadian postal service, postage prepaid, registered or certified mail, return receipt requested, or (iv) by facsimile transmission, using facsimile equipment providing written confirmation of receipt at the receiving facsimile number. All notices to the parties shall be made to the addresses provided in Exhibit A. Any notice shall be deemed to have been given on the date delivered, if delivered personally, by overnight air courier service or by facsimile transmission; or, if mailed, shall be deemed to have been given on the date shown on the return receipt as the date of delivery or the date on which the postal service certified that it was unable to deliver, whichever is applicable.

(b) Change of Address. Any party may change the address or facsimile number to which notices are to be delivered under this Agreement by giving notice of such change of address or facsimile number to the other parties in accordance with the requirements of the Section 9.1.

Sections 9.2 Entire Agreement. This Agreement contains the entire agreement and understanding of the parties with respect to the subject matter hereof and supersedes all prior agreements and understandings of the parties relating to the subject matter hereof.

Section 9.3 Amendment. This Agreement may be amended upon the consent or action in writing by Approval of the Partners.

Section 9.4 Waivers. No waiver of any provision of this Agreement shall be valid or binding unless it is in writing and signed by the parties hereto. No delay on the part of any party in exercising any right, power or privilege hereunder shall operate as a waiver thereof, nor shall any waiver of any partial exercise of any such right, power or privilege preclude any further exercise thereof or the exercise of any other such right, power or privilege. No waiver of any breach, term or condition of this Agreement by any party shall constitute a subsequent waiver of the same or any other breach, term or condition.

Section 9.5 Severable Provisions. If any provision of this Agreement shall be held invalid or unenforceable by a court of competent jurisdiction, the remainder nevertheless shall remain in full force and effect.

Section 9.6 Counterparts. This Agreement may be executed simultaneously in two or more counterparts, each of which shall be deemed an original, but all of which together shall constitute one and the same instrument.

Section 9.7 Venue; Jurisdiction. Any action or proceeding seeking to enforce any provision of, or based on any right arising out of, this Agreement may be brought against any of the parties in the courts of the State of Delaware, and each of the parties consents to the jurisdiction of such courts (and of the appropriate appellate courts) in any such action or proceeding and waives any objection to venue laid therein. Process in any action or proceeding referred to in the preceding sentence may be served on any party anywhere in the world.

Section 9.8 Governing Law. This Agreement and the rights and duties of the parties arising out of this Agreement shall be governed by, and construed in accordance with, the laws of the State of Delaware, without reference the conflict of laws rules thereof.

Section 9.9 Further Assurances. Each of the parties shall execute such agreements, instruments and other documents and take such further actions as may be reasonably required or desirable to carry out the provisions and the transactions contemplated by this Agreement, including but not limited to the execution of such further instruments of assignment, transfer, conveyance, endorsement, direction or authorization, and cooperating in obtaining any third party consent and approvals necessary in order to accomplish and give full force and effect to the transactions contemplated hereby.

Section 9.10 Successors and Assigns. Each and all of the covenants, terms, provisions and agreements herein contained shall be binding upon and inure to the benefit of the parties hereto and, to the extent permitted by this Agreement, their respective successors and assigns.

Section 9.11 Waiver of Partition. Each Partner hereby irrevocably waives during the term of the Partnership any right that it or he or she may have to maintain any action for partition with respect to any Partnership property.

[*Signature page follows*]

IN WITNESS WHEREOF, the parties hereto have caused this Agreement to be executed by their respective duly authorized representative as of the date first above written.

EPCOR POWER EQUITY LTD.

By: /s/ Kate Chisholm
Name: Kate Chisholm
Title: Vice-President and General Counsel

By: /s/ William Wright
Name: William Wright
Title: Assistant Corporate Secretary

EPLP POWER INC.

By: /s/ Kate Chisholm
Name: Kate Chisholm
Title: Vice-President and General Counsel

By: /s/ William Wright
Name: William Wright
Title: Assistant Corporate Secretary

[SIGNATURE PAGE TO AMENDED AND RESTATED PARTNERSHIP AGREEMENT OF EPCOR POWER (US) GP]

EXHIBIT A: NAMES AND ADDRESSES OF PARTNERS

All notices to the parties shall be made:

EPCOR Power Equity Ltd.
10065 Jasper Avenue
Edmonton, Alberta T5J 3B1
Attention: Executive Vice President
Telecopy No.: (780) 412-3192

EPLP Power Inc.
10065 Jasper Avenue
Edmonton, Alberta T5J 3B1
Attention: Executive Vice President
Telecopy No.: (780) 412-3192

with a copy in each instance to:

EPCOR Utilities Inc.
10065 Jasper Avenue
Edmonton, Alberta T5J 3B1
Attention: General Counsel
Telecopy No.: (780) 412-3773

EXHIBIT B
PARTNERSHIP INTEREST SCHEDULE

NAME OF PARTNER	PARTNER PERCENTAGE INTEREST	CAPITAL CONTRIBUTIONS
EPCOR Power Equity Ltd.	99.5%	$ 99,500.00
EPLP Power Inc.	0.5%	$ 500.00

EXHIBIT C
Resolution of EPCOR Power Equity Ltd. (the "Corporation") As Managing Partner of EPCOR Power (US) G.P. Resolutions of the Board of Directors (the "Board") approving the US$225 Million Private Placement

WHEREAS the Corporation, as the managing partner of the EPCOR Power (US) G.P. (the "Issuer"), has the power and authority to manage, control, administer and operate the business and affairs and to make decisions regarding the undertaking and business of the Issuer;

AND WHEREAS the Board of Directors of the Corporation (the "Board"), as managing partner of the Issuer, having been advised that the Board of Directors of EPCOR Power L.P. (the "Partnership"), the Issuer's ultimate parent, has determined that it is in the best interests of the Partnership to initiate the refinancing of existing U.S. debt facilities (the "Refinancing") and as part of the Refinancing has provided their approval to facilitate the issuance of up to US$250,000,000 in senior notes (the "Notes") of a wholly owned US subsidiary of the Partnership;

AND WHEREAS the Issuer, as part of the Refinancing, intends to conduct a private placement financing of up to US$225,000,000 of Notes, pursuant to the prior authorization of the Partnership, subject to the terms and conditions as set out on the term sheet attached to and forming part of the materials for this meeting (the "Term Sheet") and further that the Notes will be fully and unconditionally guaranteed by the Partnership (the "Offering");

AND WHEREAS the Board has been provided with a copy of the Term Sheet pursuant to which the Issuer will conduct the Offering and the net proceeds from the issuance of the Notes are to be used to refinance existing debt and/or for general purposes of the Partnership as described in the Term Sheet;

NOW, THEREFORE, upon motion duly moved and seconded, it was unanimously resolved that the following Resolutions be approved:

The Corporation, as managing partner of the Issuer, is hereby authorized to effect the Offering, as contemplated in the materials attached to the agenda for this meeting:

The Notes to be issued by the Issuer shall be issued with terms of no less than seven (7) years and no greater than fifteen (15) years with bullet repayment at maturity;

Subject to the provisions of paragraphs 1 and 2 (above), this authorization expressly extends to such non-material variations, alterations or modifications in the Offering as any two officers of the Corporation (the "Officers"), on behalf of and in its capacity as managing partner of the Issuer, determine to be necessary or desirable and in the best interests of the Issuer;

The Officers are authorized to:

(a) perform or cause to be performed on behalf of the Issuer all acts, approvals and other things to give effect to the foregoing resolutions as those persons determine to be necessary or desirable and in the best interests of the Issuer; and

(b) negotiate and settle the terms of, and execute and deliver on behalf of and in the name of the Issuer, with or without the Corporation's seal, all agreements, documents and other instruments to give effect to the foregoing resolutions as those persons determine to be necessary or desirable and in the best interests of the Issuer, and any things performed or to be performed, and any instruments executed and delivered, by those persons shall be conclusive evidence that those things and instruments have been determined by those persons to be necessary or desirable and in the best interests of the Issuer.

Any act or thing done or performed prior to the date of these resolutions, by the Officers, in relation to the Offering, to give effect to or to implement any of the foregoing resolutions, is hereby ratified, approved and confirmed.

EXHIBIT D
CERTIFICATE OF INCUMBENCY OF THE OFFICERS AND DIRECTORS OF EPCOR POWER EQUITY LTD.

I, the undersigned, of EPCOR Power Equity Ltd., hereby certify that each of the persons named below has been duly appointed to the office in EPCOR Power Equity Ltd. set opposite their respective name and that each such person is now holding such office and is acting as such officer and/or director:

NAME	OFFICE
Brian Vaasjo	*Director*
Stuart Lee	*Director*
Robert Normand	*Director*
Don Lowry	*President and Chief Executive Officer*
Mark Wiltzen	*Senior Vice President and Chief Financial Officer*
Kate Chisholm	*Vice President, General Counsel and Corporate Secretary*
John Patterson	*Vice President and Treasurer*
William Wright	*Assistant Corporate Secretary*

I give this certificate in my capacity as an officer of EPCOR Power Equity Ltd., and no personal liability is created against or assumed by me in respect of the giving of this certificate.

DATED at Edmonton, Alberta, Canada this 13th day of August, 2007.

DOCUMENT EIGHT

Statement of Partnership Authority

CA FORM: GP-1

http://bpd.cdn.sos.ca.gov/gp/forms/gp-1.pdf

"GP-1: Statement of Partnership Authority," http://bpd.cdn.sos.ca.gov/gp/forms/gp-1.pdf, State of California, 2013.

(*Continued*)

GP-1

State of California
Secretary of State

Statement of Partnership Authority

A $70.00 filing fee must accompany this form.

IMPORTANT—Read instructions before completing this form.

File # ____________________

Document # ________________

This Space For Filing Use Only

Partnership Name

1. Name of Partnership

Office Addresses (Do not abbreviate the city. Items 2 and 3 cannot be P.O. Boxes.)

2. Street Address of Chief Executive Office | City | State | Zip Code

3. Street Address of California Office, if any | City | State CA | Zip Code

4. Mailing Address of Chief Executive Office, if different from Items 2 or 3 | City | State | Zip Code

Names & Addresses of Partners (Complete Item 5 with the names and mailing addresses of all the partners (attach additional pages if necessary) **OR** leave Item 5 blank and proceed to Item 6. Any attachments to this document are incorporated herein by this reference.)

5. Name	Address	City	State	Zip Code
Name	Address	City	State	Zip Code
Name	Address	City	State	Zip Code

Appointed Agent (If Item 5 was not completed, complete Item 6 with the name and mailing address of an agent appointed and maintained by the partnership who will maintain a list of the names and mailing addresses of all the partners. If Item 5 was completed, leave Item 6 blank and proceed to Item 7.)

6. Name	Address	City	State	Zip Code

Authorized Partners (Enter the name(s) of all the partners authorized to execute instruments transferring real property held in the name of the partnership. Attach additional pages if necessary. Any attachments to this document are incorporated herein by this reference.)

7. Partner Name:	Partner Name:
Partner Name:	Partner Name
Partner Name:	Partner Name

Additional Information

8. Additional information set forth on the attached pages, if any, is incorporated herein by this reference and made part of this document.

Execution (This form must be signed by at least two partners. If additional signature space is necessary, the dated signature(s) with verification(s) may be made on an attachment to this document. Any attachments to this document are incorporated herein by this reference.)

9. I certify under penalty of perjury that the contents of this document are true.

____________________	____________________
Signature of partner	Type or Print Name of partner
____________________	____________________
Signature of partner	Type or Print Name of partner

GP-1 (REV 01/2013) APPROVED BY SECRETARY OF STATE

DOCUMENT NINE

Statement of Dissociation

CA FORM: GP-3

https://bpd.cdn.sos.ca.gov/gp/forms/gp-3.pdf

"GP-3 Statement of Dissocation," https://bpd.cdn.sos.ca.gov/gp/forms/gp-3.pdf, State of California, 2013.

(*Continued*)

Form GP-3

State of California
Secretary of State

STATEMENT OF DISSOCIATION

A $30.00 filing fee must accompany this form.
IMPORTANT—Read instructions before completing this form.

1. NAME OF PARTNERSHIP:	2. SECRETARY OF STATE FILE NUMBER:

3. NAME OF DISSOCIATED PARTNER:

4. STATEMENT THAT THE PARTNER IS DISSOCIATED FROM THE PARTNERSHIP (ATTACH ADDITIONAL PAGES IF NECESSARY):

5. NUMBER OF PAGES ATTACHED, IF ANY:

6. I DECLARE UNDER PENALTY OF PERJURY UNDER THE LAWS OF THE STATE OF CALIFORNIA THAT THE FOREGOING IS TRUE AND CORRECT.		THIS SPACE FOR FILING USE ONLY DOCUMENT # ____________
SIGNATURE OF PARTNER	DATE EXECUTED	
TYPE OR PRINT NAME OF PARTNER	COUNTY AND STATE EXECUTED	
SIGNATURE OF PARTNER	DATE EXECUTED	
TYPE OR PRINT NAME OF PARTNER	COUNTY AND STATE EXECUTED	
7. RETURN TO: NAME: ADDRESS: CITY: STATE: ZIP CODE:		

DOCUMENT TEN

Statement of Dissolution

CA FORM: GP-4

https://bpd.cdn.sos.ca.gov/gp/forms/gp-4.pdf

"GP-4 Statement of Dissolution," https://bpd.cdn.sos.ca.gov/gp/forms/gp-4.pdf, State of California, 2013.

(Continued)

Form GP-4

State of California
Secretary of State

STATEMENT OF DISSOLUTION

IMPORTANT—Read instructions before completing this form.

1. NAME OF PARTNERSHIP:	2. SECRETARY OF STATE FILE NUMBER:

3. THE ABOVE NAMED PARTNERSHIP HAS DISSOLVED AND IS WINDING UP ITS BUSINESS. (DO NOT ALTER THIS STATEMENT)

4. OTHER MATTERS, IF ANY (ATTACH ADDITIONAL PAGES IF NECESSARY):

5. NUMBER OF PAGES ATTACHED, IF ANY:

6. I DECLARE UNDER PENALTY OF PERJURY UNDER THE LAWS OF THE STATE OF CALIFORNIA THAT THE FOREGOING IS TRUE AND CORRECT.

SIGNATURE OF PARTNER	DATE EXECUTED
TYPE OR PRINT NAME OF PARTNER	COUNTY AND STATE EXECUTED
SIGNATURE OF PARTNER	DATE EXECUTED
TYPE OR PRINT NAME OF PARTNER	COUNTY AND STATE EXECUTED

7. RETURN TO:

NAME:

ADDRESS:

CITY: STATE: ZIP CODE:

THIS SPACE FOR FILING USE ONLY

DOCUMENT # ____________

SECTION III

Hybrid Entities

DOCUMENT ELEVEN

Application to Register Limited Liability Partnership

CA FORM: LLP-1

https://bpd.cdn.sos.ca.gov/llp/forms/llp-1.pdf

"LLP-1 Application to Register Limited Liability Partnership," https://bpd.cdn.sos.ca.gov/llp/forms/llp-1.pdf, State of California, 2013.

(*Continued*)

LLP-1 | **Application to Register a Limited Liability Partnership (LLP)**

To register an LLP in California, fill out this form, and submit for filing along with:

—A **$70** filing fee, and

—If the LLP is formed in another state or country, a certificate of good standing, issued within the last six (6) months by the agency where the LLP is formed.

—A separate, non-refundable **$15** service fee also must be included, **if** you drop off the completed form.

Attach extra pages if you need to include any other matters.

Important! LLPs in California may have to pay a minimum $800 yearly tax to the California Franchise Tax Board. For more information, go to https://www.ftb.ca.gov.

This Space For Office Use Only

For questions about this form, go to: *www.sos.ca.gov/business/be/filing-tips.htm*

Name to be used for this LLP in California

① ____________________

Proposed LLP Name

The name **must** end with: "Registered Limited Liability Partnership," "Limited Liability Partnership," "L.L.P.," "LLP," "R.L.L.P.," or "RLLP."

Place of Formation

② The LLP is registering as a *(check only one box)*:

a. ☐ California registered LLP formed under the laws of California.

b. ☐ Foreign LLP formed under the laws of ____________________

List the state or country where the foreign LLP is formed.

LLP Addresses

③ a. ____________________

Street Address of Principal Office | *City (no abbreviations)* | *State* | *Zip*

b. ____________________

Mailing Address of Principal Office, if different from 3a | *City (no abbreviations)* | *State* | *Zip*

Service of Process (List a California resident or an active 1505 corporation in California that agrees to be your agent to accept service of process in case the LLP is sued. You may list any adult who lives in California. You may **not** list an LLP as your agent.)

④ a. ____________________

Agent's Name

b. ____________________ ***CA***

*Agent's Street Address (if agent is **not** a corporation)* | *City (no abbreviations)* | *State* | *Zip*

Type of Business

⑤ The business in which the LLP is engaged is *(check only one box)*:

☐ The practice of Architecture ☐ The practice of Engineering ☐ The practice of Land Surveying

☐ The practice of Law ☐ The practice of Public Accountancy

☐ Related to: ____________________

List the name of the LLP to which your LLP is related, exactly as it appears on the records of the California Secretary of State. A related LLP is a California registered LLP that practices public accountancy or law, or is a foreign LLP.

Read and sign below: This form must be signed by one or more authorized partners, or if registering a foreign LLP, by a person with authority to do so under the laws of the state or country where the foreign LLP is formed. If you need more space, attach extra pages that are 1-sided and on standard letter-sized paper (8 1/2" × 11"). All attachments are part of this registration.

▶ ____________ ____________ ____________

Sign here | *Print your name here* | *Your business title*

Make check/money order payable to: **Secretary of State** Upon filing, we will return one (1) uncertified copy of your filed document for free, and will certify the copy upon request and payment of a $5 certification fee.

By Mail
Secretary of State Business Entities, P.O. Box 944228
Sacramento, CA 94244-2280

Drop-Off
Secretary of State 1500 11th Street, 3rd Floor
Sacramento, CA 95814

Corporations Code §§ 16101, 16952, 16953, 16958, 16959, Revenue and Taxation Code § 17948
LLP-1 (REV 01/2013)

2013 California Secretary of State
www.sos.ca.gov/business/be

DOCUMENT TWELVE

Certificate of Limited Partnership

CA FORM: LP-1

http://bpd.cdn.sos.ca.gov/lp/forms/lp-1.pdf

"LP-1: Certificate of Limited Partnership," http://bpd.cdn.sos.ca.gov/lp/forms/lp-1.pdf, State of California, 2019.

(Continued)

Secretary of State **Certificate of Limited Partnership (LP)**	**LP-1**

IMPORTANT—*Read Instructions* before completing this form.

Filing Fee—$70.00

Copy Fees—First page $1.00; each attachment page $0.50;
Certification Fee—$5.00

Note: LPs may have to pay minimum $800 tax to the California Franchise Tax Board each year. For more information, go to *https://www.ftb.ca.gov.*

Above Space For Office Use Only

1. Limited Partnership Name (*See Instructions* -Must contain an LP ending such as LP or L.P. "LP" will be added, if not included.)

2. Business Addresses

a. Initial Street Address of LP's Designated Office in California—Do not enter a P.O. Box	City (no abbreviations)	State **CA**	Zip Code
b. Initial Mailing Address of LP, **if different than item 2a**	City (no abbreviations)	State	Zip Code

3. Service of Process (Must provide either Individual **OR** Corporation.)
INDIVIDUAL—Complete Items 3a and 3b only. Must include agent's full name and California street address.

a. California Agent's First Name (if agent is **not** a corporation)	Middle Name	Last Name	Suffix
b. Street Address (if agent is **not** a corporation)— **Do not enter a P.O. Box**	City (no abbreviations)	State **CA**	Zip Code

CORPORATION—Complete Item 3c. Only include the name of the registered agent Corporation.

c. California Registered Corporate Agent's Name (if agent is a corporation)—Do not complete Item 3a or 3b

4. General Partners (List the name and address of each general partner. Attach additional pages, if necessary.)

a. General Partner's Name			
General Partner's Address	City (no abbreviations)	State	Zip Code
b. General Partner's Name			
General Partner's Address	City (no abbreviations)	State	Zip Code

The information contained herein, including in any attachments, is true and correct.

General Partner Signature — Type or Print Name

General Partner Signature — Type or Print Name

LP-1 (REV 06/2019)

2019 California Secretary of State
bizfile.sos.ca.gov

DOCUMENT THIRTEEN

Articles of Organization

CA FORM: LLC-1

http://bpd.cdn.sos.ca.gov/llc/forms/llc-1.pdf

"LLC-1: Articles of Organization: Limited Liability Company," https://bpd.cdn.sos.ca.gov/llc/forms/llc-1.pdf, State of California, 2019.

(Continued)

Secretary of State
Articles of Organization

LLC-1

Limited Liability Company (LLC)

IMPORTANT—Read Instructions before completing this form.

Filing Fee—$70.00

Copy Fees—First page $1.00; each attachment page $0.50; Certification Fee—$5.00

Note: LLCs may have to pay minimum $800 tax to the California Franchise Tax Board each year. For more information, go to *https://www.ftb.ca.gov.*

This Space For Office Use Only

1. Limited Liability Company Name (See Instructions—Must contain an LLC identifier such as LLC or L.L.C. "LLC" will be added, if not included.)

2. Business Addresses

a. Initial Street Address of Designated Office in California—Do not enter a P.O. Box	City (no abbreviations)	State **CA**	Zip Code
b. Initial Mailing Address of LLC, **if different than item 2a**	City (no abbreviations)	State	Zip Code

3. Service of Process (Must provide either Individual **OR** Corporation.)
INDIVIDUAL—Complete Items 3a and 3b only. Must include agent's full name and California street address.

a. California Agent's First Name (if agent is **not** a corporation)	Middle Name	Last Name	Suffix
b. Street Address (if agent is **not** a corporation)— **Do not enter a P.O. Box**	City (no abbreviations)	State **CA**	Zip Code

CORPORATION - Complete Item 3c. Only include the name of the registered agent Corporation.

c. California Registered Corporate Agent's Name (if agent is a corporation)—Do not complete Item 3a or 3b

4. Management (Select **only** one box)

The LLC will be managed by:

☐ One Manager ☐ More than One Manager ☐ All LLC Member(s)

5. Purpose Statement (Do not alter Purpose Statement)

The purpose of the limited liability company is to engage in any lawful act or activity for which a limited liability company may be organized under the California Revised Uniform Limited Liability Company Act.

6. By signing, I affirm under penalty of perjury that the information herein is true and correct and that I am authorized by California law to sign.

Additional signatures set forth on attached pages, if any, are incorporated herein by reference and made part of this Form LLC-1. (All attachments should be 8 ½ × 11, one-sided, legible and clearly marked as an attachment to this Form LLC-1.)

____________________ Organizer sign here

____________________ Print your name here

LLC-1 (REV 08/2019)

2019 California Secretary of State
bizfile.sos.ca.gov

DOCUMENT FOURTEEN

Operating Agreement (National Specialty Clinics, LLC)

S-4 2015-07-02 EX-3.140

https://www.sec.gov/Archives/edgar/data/1076863/000119312515244363/d914852dex3140.htm

Exhibit 3.140

OPERATING AGREEMENT
OF
National Specialty Clinics, LLC

A Delaware Limited Liability Company

September 30, 2009

TABLE OF CONTENTS

"Operating Agreement of National Specialty Clinics, LLC," https://www.sec.gov/Archives/edgar/data/1076863/000119312515244363/d914852dex3140.htm, U.S. Securities and Exchange Commission, 2009.

OPERATING AGREEMENT
OF
National Specialty Clinics, LLC

A Delaware Limited Liability Company

This Operating Agreement (this "***Agreement***") of **National Specialty Clinics, LLC** (the "***Company***") is made and entered into pursuant to Delaware Code (the "***Act***") and shall be effective as of September 30, 2009, by CRC Health Corporation, a Delaware corporation ("***CRC***"), as the sole member.

ARTICLE I: DEFINITIONS

For purposes of this Agreement, the following terms shall have the meanings set forth below in this Article I. The singular when used in this Agreement shall also refer to the plural, and vice versa, as appropriate. All terms used in this Agreement which are not defined in this Article I shall have the meanings set forth elsewhere in this Agreement.

"**Act**" shall mean the Delaware Code.

"**Affiliate**" shall mean, with respect to any Member: (a) any person directly or indirectly owning, controlling or holding with power to vote 10% or more of the outstanding voting securities of such Member; (b) any Person 10% or more of whose outstanding voting securities are directly or indirectly owned, controlled or held with power to vote by such Member; (c) any partnership or limited liability company of which such Member or any other Person described in clause (a) or clause (b) of this definition is a general or managing partner, or a manager, as the case may be; and (d) any officer, director or partner in such Member.

"**Agreed Value**" means the fair market value of property as determined by the Members using such reasonable methods of valuation as they deem appropriate.

"**Assignee**" shall mean a person who has acquired a beneficial interest in a Company Interest in accordance with the provisions of Article VIII hereof, but who is not a Member.

"**Book Depreciation**" means the depreciation, cost recovery or amortization of assets allowable to the Company with respect to an asset for any period, except that if the Book Value of an asset differs from its adjusted basis for federal income tax purposes at the beginning of such period, Book Depreciation shall be an amount which bears the same ratio to such beginning Book Value as federal income tax depreciation, amortization, or other cost recovery deduction for such period bears to such beginning adjusted basis.

"**Book Gain**" or "**Book Loss**" means the gain or loss that would be recognized by the Company for federal income tax purposes as a result of sales or exchanges of its assets if its tax basis in such assets were equal to the Book Value of such assets.

"**Book Value**" means (a) as to property contributed to the Company, its Agreed Value, and (b) as to all other Company property, its adjusted basis for federal income tax purposes as reflected on the books of the Company. The Book Value of all Company assets shall be adjusted to equal their respective Agreed Values, as determined by the Members, as of the following times: (a) the acquisition of an additional interest in the Company by any new or existing Member in exchange for more than a de minimis Capital Contribution; (b) the distribution by the Company to a Member of more than a de minimis amount of Company property, unless all Members receive simultaneous distributions of undivided interests in the distributed property in proportion to their Interest in the Company; and (c) the termination of the Company for federal income tax purposes pursuant to Code Section 708(b)(1)(B). The Book Value of all assets shall be adjusted by the Book Depreciation taken into account with respect to such asset.

"**Capital Account**" means an individual capital account maintained for each Member in accordance with Treasury Regulation Section 1.704-1(b) adopted pursuant to Section 704(b) of the Code.

"**Capital Contributions**" shall mean the amount of cash or Book Value of property a Member contributes to the capital of the Company.

"**Certificate**" shall mean the certificate of formation of the Company which is required to be filed pursuant to the Act.

"**Code**" shall mean the Internal Revenue Code of 1986, as amended from time to time, and the corresponding provisions of any future Federal tax law and, to the extent applicable, the Regulations.

"**Company Interest**," as of any date, shall mean, with respect to any Member, the percentage ownership interest of such Member in the Company as of such date, including all of its rights and obligations under the Act and this Agreement. Each Member's Company Interest shall be represented by the number of Units set forth on Exhibit A attached hereto.

"**Distributions**" means all cash and the Book Value of other property distributed to NSC arising from its Company Interest.

"**Fiscal Year**" shall mean the fiscal year of the Company which shall be the calendar year.

"**Initial Member**" shall mean CRC Health Corporation.

"**Manager**" shall mean initially CRC Health Management, Inc., a Delaware corporation, or such other Person as the Member may later appoint.

"**Member**" shall mean the Initial Member and any other Person that acquires a Company Interest and is admitted to the Company as a member in accordance with the terms of this Agreement.

"**Net Income**" or "**Net Loss**" shall mean, with respect to any fiscal period, the gross income, gains and losses of the Company, for such period, less all deductible costs, expenses and depreciation and amortization allowances of the Company for such period, as determined for federal income tax purposes, with the following adjustments: (a) any income of the Company that is exempt from federal income tax and is not otherwise taken into account in computing Net Income or Net Loss pursuant to this definition shall be added to such taxable income or loss; (b) any expenditures of the Company not deductible in computing taxable income or loss, not properly chargeable to capital account and not otherwise taken into account in computing Net Income or Net Loss pursuant to this definition shall be subtracted from such taxable income or loss; (c) if the Book Value of any asset differs from its adjusted basis for federal income tax purposes at the beginning of such period, the depreciation and amortization allowances to be deducted from gross income with respect to such asset shall be Book Depreciation; and (d) Book Gain or Book Loss shall be used instead of taxable gain or loss. If such amount shall be greater than zero, it shall be known as a "**Net Income**" and if such amount shall be less than zero, it shall be known as "**Net Loss.**"

"**Person**" shall mean an individual, partnership, joint venture, association, corporation, trust, estate, limited liability company, limited liability partnership or any other legal entity.

"**Regulations**" shall mean the regulations, including temporary regulations promulgated under the Code, as such regulations may be amended from time to time (including the corresponding provisions of any future regulations).

"**Units**" shall mean the number of units representing the Company Interest held by a Member. Each Unit shall represent 1% of the total outstanding Company Interest.

ARTICLE II: CONTINUATION AND PURPOSE

2.01 Formation. The Initial Member hereby organizes a limited liability company pursuant to the Act. The rights and liabilities of the Members shall be determined pursuant to the Act and this Agreement. To the extent that the rights or obligations of the Members are different by reason of any provision of this Agreement than they would be in the absence of such provision, this Agreement shall, to the extent permitted by the Act, control. Simultaneously with the execution and delivery of this Agreement, NSC shall be admitted as the sole member of the Company.

2.02 Limited Liability Company Agreement. This Agreement shall constitute the "limited liability company agreement" of the Company within the meaning of the Act for all purposes including, without limitation, so long as there is only one Member, for classification of the Company as a "domestic eligible entity" that is disregarded as an entity separate from its owner for federal and all relevant state income tax purposes.

2.03 Name. The name of the Company is stated in the preamble.

2.04 Principal Office. The registered office required to be maintained by the Company in the state of West Virginia pursuant to the Act shall initially be located at c/o National Registered Agents, Inc. 300 Kanawha Blvd., Charleston, WV 24321. The registered agent shall initially be National Registered Agents, Inc. 300 Kanawha Blvd., Charleston, WV 25321. The principal executive office of the Company shall be at 20400 Stevens Creek Blvd., Suite 600, Cupertino, California 95014.

2.05 Term. The term of the Company commenced on the date of filing of the Certificate with the Secretary of State of West Virginia, and shall continue unless terminated as hereinafter provided.

2.06 Purposes of Company. The Company is permitted to engage in any lawful acts or activities and to exercise any powers permitted to limited liability companies under the laws of the State of West Virginia.

2.07 Certificate. The Manager shall cause the Certificate to be filed or recorded in any other public office where filing or recording is required.

2.08 Address of the Initial Member. The address of the Initial Member is 20400 Stevens Creek Blvd., Suite 600, Cupertino, California 95014.

2.09 Foreign Qualification. The Manager shall take all necessary actions to cause the Company to be qualified to conduct business legally in any jurisdictions where the nature of the Company's business requires such qualification.

ARTICLE III: MEMBERS' CAPITAL

3.01 Capital Contribution. The Members shall be obligated to make only such capital contributions to the Company as the Members shall agree to in writing. The Initial Member shall be credited with one hundred percent (100%) of the existing capital of the Company.

3.02 Additional Capital Contributions. The Members shall not be required to contribute additional capital to the Company. The Members shall not be obligated to restore any deficit balance in their Capital Accounts.

ARTICLE IV: STATUS OF MEMBERS AND MANAGER

4.01 Limited Liability. Neither the Members nor the Manager shall be bound by or personally liable for the expenses, liabilities or obligations of the Company. Except as required by the Act, the debts, obligations and liabilities of the Company, whether arising in contract, tort or otherwise, shall be solely the debts, obligations and liabilities of the Company, and neither the Members nor the Manager shall be obligated personally for any such debt, obligation or liability of the Company solely by reason of being a

Member or acting as the Manager of the Company. The Members shall be liable to the Company for the capital contributions specified in Section 3.01 and as may otherwise be required pursuant to the Act. Neither the Members nor the Manager shall be liable for any debts, obligations and liabilities, whether arising in contract, tort or otherwise, of any other Member or any Manager of the Company. The Members shall not be required to loan the Company any funds.

4.02 Return of Distributions of Capital. A Member may, under certain circumstances, be required by law to return to the Company for the benefit of the Company's creditors, amounts previously distributed. No Member shall be obligated to pay those distributions to or for the account of the Company or any creditor of the Company. However, if any court of competent jurisdiction holds that, notwithstanding the provisions of this Agreement, any Member is obligated to return or pay over any part of those distributions, it shall be the obligation of such Member. Any payment returned to the Company or made directly by a Member to a creditor of the Company shall be deemed a Capital Contribution by such Member.

4.03 Reliance by Third Parties. Persons dealing with the Company are entitled to rely conclusively upon the power and authority of the Manager as set forth in this Agreement.

ARTICLE V: COMPENSATION TO THE MEMBERS AND MANAGER

Neither the Members nor the Manager shall receive any compensation directly or indirectly in connection with the formation, operation, and dissolution of the Company except as expressly specified in this Agreement.

ARTICLE VI: COMPANY EXPENSES

6.01 Reimbursement. The Company shall reimburse the Members for all out-of-pocket costs and expenses reasonably incurred by it in connection with the operation and funding of the Company, including any legal fees and expenses.

6.02 Operating Expenses. The Company shall pay the operating expenses of the Company which may include, but are not limited to: (i) all reasonable salaries, compensation and fringe benefits of personnel employed by the Company and involved in the business of the Company; (ii) all costs of funds borrowed by the Company and all taxes and other assessments on the Company's assets and other taxes applicable to the Company; (iii) reasonable legal, audit and accounting fees; (iv) the cost of insurance as required in connection with the business of the Company; (v) reasonable expenses of revising, amending, or modifying this Agreement or terminating the Company; (vi) reasonable expenses in connection with distributions made by the Company, and communications necessary in maintaining relations with Members and outside parties, (vii) reasonable expenses in connection with preparing and mailing reports required to be furnished to Members for investor, tax reporting or other purposes, or other reports to Members; (viii) reasonable costs incurred in connection with any litigation in which the Company is involved, as well as any examination, investigation or other proceedings conducted by any regulatory agency with jurisdiction over the Company, including legal and accounting fees incurred in connection therewith; (ix) property management fees; and (x) reasonable expenses of professionals employed by the Company in connection with any of the foregoing, including attorneys, accountants and appraisers.

ARTICLE VII: ALLOCATION OF INCOME AND LOSS; DISTRIBUTIONS

7.01 Distributions. All Distributions shall be paid to the Initial Member. If there is more than one Member, the Members shall amend this Section 7.01 to reflect the Members' agreement regarding payment of Distributions.

7.02 Allocations of Net Income and Net Losses. Net Income and Net Losses of the Company for each Fiscal Year shall be allocated 100% to the Initial Member. If there is more than one Member, the Members shall amend this Section 7.02 to reflect the Members' agreement regarding allocation of Net Income and Net Losses of the Company.

ARTICLE VIII: ASSIGNMENT OF COMPANY INTERESTS

8.01 Assignment. A Member may assign (whether by sale, exchange, gift contribution, distribution or other transfer, including a pledge or other assignment for security purposes) all or any part of its Company Interest.

8.02 Assignee. Provided the provisions of this Article VIII have been complied with, an Assignee shall be entitled to receive distributions of cash or other property, and allocations of Net Income and Net Losses, from the Company attributable to the assigned Company Interests from and after the effective date of the assignment in accordance with Article VII, but an Assignee shall have no other rights of a Member herein, such as rights to any information, an accounting, inspection of books or records or voting as a Member on matters set forth herein or by law, until such Assignee is admitted as a Member pursuant to the provisions of Article X; except that an Assignee shall have the right solely to receive a copy of the annual financial statements required herein to be provided the Members. The Company shall be entitled to treat the assignor as the absolute owner of the Company Interests in all respects, and shall incur no liability for distributions, allocations of Net Income or Net Losses, or transmittal of reports and notices required to be given to Members which are made in good faith to the assignor until the effective date of the assignment, or, in the case of the transmittal of reports (other than the financial statements referred to above) or notices, until the Assignee is so admitted as a substitute Member. The effective date of an assignment shall be the first day of the calendar month following the month in which the Member has received an executed instrument of assignment in compliance with this Article VIII or the first day of a later month if specified in the executed instrument of assignment. The Assignee shall be deemed an Assignee on the effective date, and shall be only entitled to distributions, Net Income or Net Losses attributable to the period after the effective date of assignment. Each Assignee will inherit the balance of the Capital Account, as of the effective date of Assignment, of the Assignor with respect to the Company Interest transferred.

8.03 Collateral Assignment. Notwithstanding anything to the contrary in the foregoing Section 8.02 and to the extent permitted by the Act, in the event a Member pledges its Company Interest or its Units, or assigns its Company Interests or its Units for security purposes, or otherwise encumbers its Company Interest or its Units, to a Member's lenders that provide financing to such Member (the "**Lenders**"), (i) such Member may physically deliver the certificate or certificates representing its Units to its Lenders; (ii) the provisions of Article X shall not apply to the admission of any such Lender as a Member upon the exercise by such Lender of any rights and remedies under any of the Member's agreements with such Lender; (iii) such Lender shall be entitled to become a member of the Company and otherwise effect the transfer of the assigning Member's Company Interest and Units to such Lender or such other Person as Lender may select consistent with the terms of the Member's agreements with such Lender upon the exercise by such Lender of any rights and remedies under any of the Member's agreements with such Lender, and such

Lender or other Person may thereafter exercise all rights and other entitlements of membership in the Company pertaining thereto, in all cases without being required to comply with the provisions of Article X or to make any required Capital Contributions; and (iv) such Lenders or other Persons to whom the Company Interest or Units are transferred by Lender shall be deemed Members without further action upon the effectiveness of such transfer.

8.04 Other Consents and Requirements. Any assignment, sale, transfer, exchange or other disposition of any Company Interest in the Company or the Units must be in compliance with any requirements imposed by any state securities administrator having jurisdiction over the assignment, sale, transfer, exchange or other disposition of the Company Interest or the Units, and the United States Securities and Exchange Commission.

ARTICLE IX: ISSUANCE OF UNIT CERTIFICATES

9.01 Unit Certificates. Each Member shall be issued a certificate or certificates for Units to denominate such Member's Company Interest. The names of each Member and the number of Units held by such Member, together with the certificate number of each Unit certificate issued to such Member shall be set forth on Exhibit A attached hereto. All certificates shall be signed in the name of the Company by the President and the Chief Financial Officer or Secretary of the Manager, certifying the number of Units owned by the Unit holder. Any or all of the signatures on a certificate may be by facsimile signature.

9.02 Restrictive Legend. In order to reflect the restrictions on disposition of the Units as set forth in this Agreement, the certificates for the Units will be endorsed with a restrictive legend, including without limitation one or both of the following:

> "THE UNITS REPRESENTED BY THIS CERTIFICATE HAVE NOT BEEN REGISTERED UNDER THE SECURITIES ACT OF 1933, AS AMENDED, OR UNDER ANY STATE SECURITIES LAWS, AND MAY BE OFFERED AND SOLD ONLY IF SO REGISTERED OR AN EXEMPTION FROM REGISTRATION IS AVAILABLE. THE HOLDER OF THESE UNITS MAY BE REQUIRED TO DELIVER TO THE COMPANY, IF THE COMPANY SO REQUESTS, AN OPINION OF COUNSEL (REASONABLY SATISFACTORY IN FORM AND SUBSTANCE TO THE COMPANY) TO THE EFFECT THAT AN

EXEMPTION FROM REGISTRATION UNDER THE SECURITIES ACT (OR QUALIFICATION UNDER STATE SECURITIES LAWS) IS AVAILABLE WITH RESPECT TO ANY TRANSFER OF THESE UNITS THAT HAS NOT BEEN SO REGISTERED (OR QUALIFIED).

THE COMPANY WILL FURNISH WITHOUT CHARGE TO EACH HOLDER WHO SO REQUESTS THE POWERS, DESIGNATIONS, PREFERENCES AND RELATIVE RIGHTS OF THE UNITS. THE UNITS EVIDENCED HEREBY ARE SUBJECT TO AN OPERATING AGREEMENT (A COPY OF WHICH MAY BE OBTAINED UPON WRITTEN REQUEST FROM THE COMPANY). FOR ALL PURPOSES, THIS CERTIFICATE AND THE UNITS IT REPRESENTS SHALL BE DEEMED A SECURITY OR SECURITIES GOVERNED BY ARTICLE VIII OF THE UNIFORM COMMERCIAL CODE."

9.03 Additional Legends. If required by the authorities of any state in connection with the issuance of the Units, the legend or legends required by such state authorities shall also be endorsed on all such certificates.

9.04 Lost Certificates. Except as provided in this Section 9.04, no new certificate for Units shall be issued in lieu of an old certificate unless the latter is surrendered to the Company and canceled at the same time. The Company may, in case any Unit certificate or certificates is lost, stolen or destroyed, authorize the issuance of a new certificate in lieu thereof, upon such terms and conditions as the Company may require, including provision for indemnification of the Company sufficient to protect the Company against any claim that may be made against it, including any expense or liability, on account of the alleged loss, theft or destruction of such certificate or the issuance of such new certificate.

9.05 Uniform Commercial Code. For all purposes under this Agreement and any agreement between the Company and its lenders, all of the Company Interests in the Company and the Units issued by the Company representing the same shall be deemed a security or securities governed by Article VIII of the Uniform Commercial Code.

ARTICLE X: ADMISSION OF ASSIGNEE AS MEMBER

10.01 Requirements. An Assignee may not become a Member unless all of the following conditions are first satisfied:

(a) A duly executed and acknowledged written instrument of assignment is filed with the Company, specifying the Company Interest and the Units being assigned and setting forth the intention of the Assignor that the Assignee succeed to Assignor's interest as a substitute Member;

(b) The Assignor and Assignee shall execute and acknowledge any other instruments that the Company deems necessary or desirable for substitution, including the written acceptance and adoption by the Assignee of the provisions of this Agreement;
(c) The admission of the Assignee is approved by the Members;
(d) Payment of a transfer fee to the Company, sufficient to cover all reasonable expenses connected with the substitution; and
(e) Compliance with Article VIII of this Agreement.

10.02 Issuance of Unit Certificates to Assignees. An Assignee shall be issued a certificate or certificates for the Units it acquires upon satisfaction of the requirements set forth in Section 10.01 and compliance with the requirements of Section 9.04.

ARTICLE XI: BOOKS, RECORDS, ACCOUNTING AND REPORTS

11.01 Books and Records. The Company shall maintain at its principal office all of the following:

(a) A current list of the full name and last known business or residence address of each Member set forth in alphabetical order together with the Capital Contributions and Company Interest owned by each Member;
(b) A copy of the Certificate, this Agreement and any and all amendments to either thereof, together with executed copies of any powers of attorney pursuant to which any certificate or amendment has been executed;
(c) Copies of the Company's federal, state and local income tax or information returns and reports, if any, for the six most recent taxable years;
(d) The financial statements of the Company for the six most recent fiscal years;
(e) The Company books and records for at least the current and past three fiscal years.

11.02 Delivery to Members and Inspection.

(a) Upon the request of a Member, the Company shall promptly deliver to the requesting Member a copy of the information required to be maintained by Section 11.01, except for Section 11.01(e).

(b) Each Member, or his duly authorized representative, has the right, upon reasonable request, to each of the following:

(1) Inspect and copy during normal business hours any of the Company records; and

(2) Obtain from the Company, promptly after becoming available, a copy of the Company's federal, state and local income tax or information returns for each year.

(c) The Company shall send to each Member within eighty-five (85) days after the end of each Fiscal Year the information necessary for the Member to complete its federal and state income tax or information returns. The Company shall use its best efforts to send to each Member such information within seventy-five (75) days after the end of each Fiscal Year.

11.03 Annual Statements. The Company shall cause to be prepared for the Members at least annually, at Company expense financial statements of the Company. The financial statements will include a balance sheet, statements of income or loss, cash flows and Members' equity.

11.04 Bank Accounts. The Company shall maintain appropriate accounts at one or more financial institutions for all funds of the Company as determined by the Manager. Such accounts shall be used solely for the business of the Company. Withdrawals from such accounts shall be made only upon the signature of those persons authorized by the Manager.

11.05 Tax Returns. The Manager shall cause any federal, state or local income tax returns of the Company to be prepared and filed on behalf of the Company, and it shall cause copies of such returns to be furnished to each of the Members.

11.06 Disregarded Entity for Federal and State Income and Franchise Tax Purposes. The Initial Member intends that, so long as there is only one Member, the Company shall be treated as a "domestic eligible entity" that is disregarded as an entity separate from its owner (a "Disregarded Entity") for federal, state and local income and franchise tax purposes and shall take all reasonable action, including the amendment of this Agreement and the execution of other documents but without changing the economic relationships created by, or the essential terms of, this Agreement, as may be reasonably required to qualify for and receive treatment as a Disregarded Entity for federal income tax purposes.

ARTICLE XII: DESIGNATION OF RIGHTS, AUTHORITIES, POWERS, RESPONSIBILITIES, DUTIES AND LIMITATIONS OF THE MANAGER

12.01 Authority of Manager.

(a) The Manager shall have the exclusive authority to manage the operations and affairs of the Company, shall have the power on behalf and in the name of the Company to carry out any and all of the objects and purposes of the Company, and shall have all authority, rights, and powers conferred by law and those required or appropriate for the management of the Company business.

(b) The Members agree that all determinations, decisions, and actions made or taken by the Manager in accordance with this Agreement shall be conclusive and absolutely binding upon the Company, the Members and their respective successors, assigns and personal representatives.

12.02 Acts of Manger. The Manager is the agent of the Company for the purpose of its business, and the acts of the Manger in carrying on the usual business of the Company shall bind the Company, unless (1) the Manager has in fact no authority to act on behalf of the Company in the particular matter, and (2) the person with whom the Manager is dealing has knowledge of the fact that the Manager has no such authority.

12.03 Expenses. The Company will pay, or will reimburse the Manager for all costs and expenses incurred by the Manager in connection with the organization and operations of the Company.

12.04 Matters Requiring Consent. Notwithstanding any other provision of this Agreement to the contrary, actions or decisions with respect to any of the following matters shall require the prior written consent of the Initial Member:

(a) amendment of this Agreement, the Certificate or other organizational documents of the Company;

(b) the admission of additional Members to the Company;

(c) the voluntary bankruptcy or entering into receivership of the Company;

(d) the sale or exchange, or other disposition or transfer of all or substantially all of the assets of the Company;

(e) approval of any merger, consolidation, exchange or reclassification of interest or shares involving the Company, or any other form of reorganization or recapitalization involving the Company;

(f) the dissolution or liquidation of the Company other than as set forth in this Agreement; and

(g) any approval by the Company of any assignment or other transfer, whether voluntarily, involuntarily or by operation of law, by any person of such person's rights, obligations or duties under any agreement between such person and the Company, consent to which by the Initial Member may be given or withheld in the sole and absolute discretion of the Initial Member.

12.05 Officers.

(a) The Manager may appoint officers of the Company at any time. The officers of the Company, if deemed necessary by the Manager may include a president, one or more vice presidents, secretary and one or more assistant secretaries, and chief financial officer (and one or more assistant treasurers). Any individual may hold any number of offices. The officers shall exercise such powers and perform such duties as specified in this Agreement and as shall be determined from time to time by the Manager.

(b) Subject to the rights, if any, of an officer under a contract of employment, any officer may be removed, either with or without cause, by the Manager at any time. Any officer may resign at any time by giving written notice to the Company. Any resignation shall take effect at the date of the receipt of that notice or at any later time specified in that notice; and, unless otherwise specified in that notice, the acceptance of the resignation shall not be necessary to make it effective. Any resignation is without prejudice to the rights, if any, of the Company under any contract to which the officer is a party. A vacancy in any office because of death, resignation, removal, disqualification or any other cause shall be filled in the manner prescribed in this Agreement for regular appointments to that office.

(c) The president shall be the chief executive officer of the Company, and shall, subject to the control of the Manager, have general and active management of the business of the Company and shall see that all orders and resolutions of the Manager are carried into effect. The president shall have the general powers and duties of management usually vested in the office of president of a corporation, and shall have such other powers and duties as may be prescribed by a Manager or this Agreement. The president shall execute bonds, mortgages and other contracts requiring a seal, under the seal of the Company, except where required or permitted by law to be otherwise signed and executed, and except where the signing and execution thereof shall be expressly delegated by the Manager to some other officer or agent of the Company.

(d) The vice-president, or if there shall be more than one, the vice-presidents in the order determined by the Manager, shall, in the absence or disability of the president, perform the duties and exercise the powers of the president and shall perform such other duties and have such other powers as the Manager may from time to time prescribe.

(e) The secretary shall attend all meetings of the Members, and shall record all the proceedings of the meeting in a book to be kept for that purpose and shall perform like duties for the standing committees when required. The secretary shall give or cause to be given, notice of all meetings of the Members and shall perform such other duties as may be prescribed by the Manager. The secretary shall have custody of the seal, if any, of the Company and the Secretary shall have authority to affix the same to any instrument requiring it, and when so affixed, it may he attested by his or her signature. The secretary shall keep, or cause to be kept at the principal executive office or at the office of the Company's transfer agent or registrar, as determined by the Manager, all documents described in Section 11.01 and such other documents as may be required under the Act. The secretary shall perform such other duties and have such other authority as may be prescribed elsewhere in this Agreement or from time to time by the Manager. The secretary shall have the general duties, powers and responsibilities of a secretary of a corporation.

(f) The chief financial officer shall keep and maintain, or cause to be kept and maintained, adequate and correct books and records of accounts of the properties and business transactions of the Company, including accounts of its assets, liabilities, receipts, disbursements, gains, losses, Capital Accounts and Company Interests. The chief financial officer shall have the custody of the funds and securities of the Company, and shall keep full and accurate accounts of receipts and disbursements in books belonging to the Company, and shall deposit all moneys and other valuable effects in the name and to the credit of the Company in such depositories as may be designated by the Manager. The chief financial officer shall disburse the funds of the Company as may be ordered by the Manager. The chief financial officer shall perform such other duties and shall have such other responsibility and authority as may be prescribed elsewhere in this Agreement from time to time by the Manager.

The chief financial officer shall have the general duties, powers and responsibilities of a chief financial officer of a corporation, and shall be the chief financial and accounting officer of the Company.

ARTICLE XIII: RIGHTS, POWERS AND VOTING RIGHTS OF THE MEMBERS

13.01 Request for Vote. In the event there is more than one Member, any Member holding in the aggregate a Company Interest which equals or exceeds five percent (5%) may call a meeting of the Members for a vote, or may call for a vote without a meeting. In either event, such Member shall establish a date for the meeting on which votes shall be counted and shall mail by first class mail a notice to all Members of the time and place of the Company meeting, if called, and the general nature of the business to be transacted, or if no such meeting has been called, of the matter or matters to be voted and the date which the votes will be counted.

13.02 Procedures. In the event there is more than one Member, each Member shall be entitled to cast one vote for each full Unit held of record by such Member: (i) at a meeting, in person, by written proxy or by a signed writing directing the manner in which he desires that his vote be cast, which writing must be received by the Company prior to such meeting, or (ii) without a meeting, by a signed writing directing the manner in which he desires that his vote be cast, which writing must be received by the Company prior to the date on which the votes of Members are to be counted. Only the votes of Members of record on the notice date, whether at a meeting or otherwise, shall be counted.

13.03 Action by Consent. Notwithstanding anything to the contrary contained in this Article XIII, any action or approval required or permitted by this Agreement to be taken or given by the Initial Member or at any meeting of Members (whether by vote or consent), may be taken or given without a meeting, without prior notice and without a vote, if a consent in writing, setting forth the action so taken or approval so given, shall be signed by the Initial Member, or if there is more than one Member, by Members owning Company Interests having not less than the minimum number of votes that would be necessary to authorize or take such action or give such approval at a meeting at which all Members entitled to vote thereon were present and voted. Prompt notice of the taking of any action or the giving of any approval without a meeting by less than unanimous written consent shall be given to those Members who have not consented in writing.

ARTICLE XIV: DISSOLUTION OF THE COMPANY

14.01 Termination of Membership. No Member shall resign from the Company, or take any voluntary action to commence bankruptcy proceedings or dissolve itself. The bankruptcy of a Member shall not be considered a withdrawal by such Member from the Company and such Member shall continue to be a Member of the Company. If any Member ceases to be a Member for any reason, the business of the Company shall be continued by the remaining Members, provided, however, if there are no remaining Members, the successor in interest to the last remaining Member may elect to continue the business.

14.02 Events of Dissolution or Liquidation. The Company shall be dissolved upon the happening of any of the following events:

(a) The failure of the successor-in-interest to the last remaining Member to continue the Company in accordance with the provisions of Section 14.01 hereof after the termination of such Member's membership;
(b) The sale, exchange, or other disposition or transfer of all or substantially all of the assets of the Company;
(c) Upon the unanimous consent of the Members; or
(d) Subject to any provision of this Agreement that limits or prevents dissolution, the happening of any event that, under the Act caused the dissolution of a limited liability company.

14.03 Liquidation. Upon dissolution of the Company for any reason, the Company shall immediately commence to wind up its affairs. A reasonable period of time shall be allowed for the orderly termination of the Company business, discharge of its liabilities and distribution or liquidation of the remaining assets so as to enable the Company to minimize the normal losses attendant to the liquidation process. A full accounting of the assets and liabilities of the Company shall be taken and a statement thereof shall be furnished to each Member within thirty (30) days after the dissolution. Such accounting and statements shall be prepared under the direction of the Member or, by a liquidating trustee selected by unanimous consent of the Members. The Company property and assets and/or the proceeds from the liquidation thereof shall be applied in the following order of priority:

(a) First, payment of the debts and liabilities of the Company, in the order of priority provided by law (including any loans by the Members to the Company) and payment of the expenses of liquidation;
(b) Second, setting up of such reserves as the Manager or liquidating trustee may deem reasonably necessary for any contingent or unforeseen liabilities or obligations of the Company or any obligation or liability not then due and payable; provided, however, that any such reserve shall be paid over by the Manager or liquidating trustee to an escrow agent, to be held by such escrow agent for the purpose of disbursing such reserves in payment of such liabilities, and, at the expiration of such escrow period as the Manager or liquidating trustee shall deem advisable but not to exceed one calendar year, to distribute the balance thereafter remaining in the manner hereinafter provided; and
(c) Third, to the Members in accordance with the provisions of Section 7.01.

14.04 Certificate of Cancellation. As soon as possible (but in no event later than 90 days) following the completion of the winding up of the Company, the Manager (or any other appropriate representative of the Company) shall execute a certificate of cancellation in the form prescribed by the Act and shall file the same with the office of the Secretary of State of the State of West Virginia.

ARTICLE XV: MISCELLANEOUS

15.01 Severability. If any term or provision of this Agreement is held illegal, invalid or unenforceable, such illegality, invalidity or unenforceability shall not affect the legality, validity or enforceability of the remainder of this Agreement.

15.02 General. This Agreement: (i) shall be binding on the executors, administrators, estates, heirs and legal successors of the Members and Manager; (ii) be governed by and construed in accordance with the laws of the State of West Virginia (without regard to principles of conflict of laws); (iii) may be executed in more than one counterpart as of the day and year first above written; and (iv) contains the entire limited liability company agreement with respect to the Company. The waiver of any of the provisions, terms or conditions contained in this Agreement shall not be considered as a waiver of any of the other provisions, terms or conditions hereof.

15.03 Notices, Etc. All notices and other communications required or permitted hereunder shall be in writing and shall be deemed effectively given upon personal delivery, confirmation of telex or telecopy, or upon the fifth day following mailing by registered mail, postage prepaid, addressed (a) if to any Member at such addresses as set forth on the records of the Company, or at such other address as any Member shall have furnished to the Company in writing, (b) if to the Company or the Manager, at 20400 Stevens Creek Blvd., Suite 600, Cupertino, California 95014.

15.04 Amendment. This Agreement may only be modified or amended if approved by all of the Members.

[Signature page follows.]

IN WITNESS WHEREOF, the undersigned has adopted this Operating Agreement as of the day and year first set forth above.

MEMBER: **CRC Health Corporation,**
a Delaware corporation
By: /s/ Kevin Hogge
Kevin Hogge
Chief Financial Officer

ACKNOWLEDGED AND AGREED:
MANAGER: **CRC Health Management, Inc.,**
a Delaware corporation

By: /s/ Kevin Hogge
Kevin Hogge
Chief Financial Officer

EXHIBIT A
MEMBERS

MEMBER	MEMBER'S COMPANY INTEREST	NUMBER OF UNITS	CERTIFICATE NUMBER
CRC Health Corporation	100%	100	1

DOCUMENT FIFTEEN

Certificate of Dissolution

CA FORM: LLC-3

http://bpd.cdn.sos.ca.gov/llc/forms/llc-3--4-7.pdf

"LLC-3: Certificate of Dissolution," http://bpd.cdn.sos.ca.gov/llc/forms/llc-3--4-7.pdf, State of California, 2019.

(*Continued*)

Secretary of State **Certificate of Dissolution** **Limited Liability Company (LLC)** (California LLC ONLY)	**LLC-3**
IMPORTANT—Read Instructions before completing this form. There is **No Fee** for filing a Certificate of Dissolution **Copy Fees**—First page $1.00; each attachment page $0.50; Certification Fee—$5.00 plus copy fees	**This Space For Office Use Only**

1. **Limited Liability Company Name** (Enter the exact name of the LLC as it is recorded with the California Secretary of State)

2. **LLC 12-Digit Entity (File) Number** (Enter the exact 12-digit Entity (File) Number issued by the California Secretary of State.)

3. **Dissolution** (Check the applicable statement. This Form LLC-3 is not required when the vote to dissolve was made by all of the members and that fact is noted on the Certificate of Cancellation (Form LLC-4/7).)

The dissolution of this LLC was caused by one of the following circumstances (**check one**):

☐ The happening of an event as set forth in the Articles of Organization or in the LLC's written Operating Agreement.

☐ The vote of 50 percent or more of the voting interests of the members of the LLC or a greater percentage of the voting interests of members as specified in the Articles of Organization or written Operating Agreement.

☐ The passage of 90 consecutive days during which the LLC has no members, except on the death of a natural person who is the sole member of the LLC, the status of the member, including a membership interest, may pass to the heirs, successors and assigns of the member by will or applicable law.

☐ The entry of a decree of judicial dissolution pursuant to California Corporations Code section 17707.03.

The Certificate of Dissolution puts all on notice that the LLC has elected to wind up the business of the LLC and is in the process of paying liabilities and distributing assets. In order to terminate the LLC, the LLC also **must file a Certificate of Cancellation (Form LLC-4/7)**.

4. **Read and Sign Below (See instructions for signature requirements**. Do not use a computer generated signature.)

By signing, I affirm under penalty of perjury that the information herein is true and correct and that I am authorized by California law to sign.

Signature	Type or Print Name
Signature	Type or Print Name

LLC-3 (REV 08/2019)

2019 California Secretary of State
bizfile.sos.ca.gov

www.ingramcontent.com/pod-product-compliance
Ingram Content Group UK Ltd.
Pitfield, Milton Keynes, MK11 3LW, UK
UKHW051452290926
15471UKWH00008B/1160

9 781793 526830